JANE JACOBS

JANE JACOBS
THE LAST INTERVIEW
and OTHER CONVERSATIONS

MELVILLE HOUSE
BROOKLYN • LONDON

Melville House Publishing   8 Blackstock Mews
46 John Street   and   Islington
Brooklyn, NY 11201   London N4 2BT

mhpbooks.com   facebook.com/mhpbooks   @melvillehouse

Library of Congress Control Number: 2016933877

ISBN: 978-1-61219-534-6

Printed in the United States of America

1   3   5   7   9   10   8   6   4   2

CONTENTS

DISTURBER OF THE PEACE: JANE JACOBS

INTERVIEW BY EVE AUCHINCLOSS AND NANCY LYNCH
MADEMOISELLE
OCTOBER 1962

Jane Jacobs, a former associate editor of *Architectural Forum*, is the author of a vigorous attack on the dogmas of urban redevelopment called *The Death and Life of Great American Cities*. Since its publication a year ago, it has been much argued and discussed. City planners tend to be highly critical, but people who feel that our cities are being dehumanized have responded enthusiastically to her fresh and imaginative ideas. Diversity, she believes, is the source of urban vitality, and it is achieved by mixtures of residences, business, and industry, of old and new buildings, of rich and poor; of busy streets with short blocks and of many people living together. No matter how they like her assumptions, everyone agrees that she has started something. For the first time in generations, new ideas about what makes a city work are being discussed and even, tentatively, applied. This is the ninth in *Mademoiselle*'s series of taped interviews, "Disturbers of the Peace."

· · ·

AUCHINCLOSS AND LYNCH: If cities are to help us lead a good life, what should they be like?

JACOBS: Well, they have to be very fertile places economically and socially, for the plans of thousands and tens of thousands of people.

AUCHINCLOSS AND LYNCH: And do you think that proper cities can make for a creative life?

JACOBS: They can in the sense that big cities offer the greatest range of opportunity for people with unusual wares or new ideas. It takes a great big city to support either commerce or culture that isn't absolutely standardized. And if we have big cities that are unable to offer services, then we are not getting the salient advantages. What's the point of having the disadvantages—and they do exist—and none of the advantages?

AUCHINCLOSS AND LYNCH: But look at the foolish kinds of specialization you get. In New York all the art, for instance, is stuffed into two or three museums instead of being dispersed. The Whitney used to be downtown, but now it's just an annex of the Museum of Modern Art.

JACOBS: The idea of officially lumping all like things together is ridiculous. I'm convinced people go to the Whitney as an afterthought. When it was in a place by itself people went to see what was there.

AUCHINCLOSS AND LYNCH: How could you start a reverse process?

JACOBS: These things don't happen inevitably. All this segregation has been deliberately prescribed—like the mammoth museums, the Lincoln Centers, the housing projects. Extraordinary powers of government have been created to make possible such islands of single use, because it was thought that this is the way to organize cities. It's not just a matter of reversing the process, though, because mere planlessness isn't enough. We have bad unplanned areas as well as bad planned ones. Change will come about—and I believe it will—first from understanding the problem a city is, and then changing the methods of dealing with it. But there's a step before that, and this sounds negative, but I think we won't really get things done differently and better until citizen resistance makes it impossible—or too frustrating—to do things as they are being done now.

AUCHINCLOSS AND LYNCH: How bad will things have to get before the rebellion begins?

JACOBS: I think it's started, not just in New York, but in many other big cities—Chicago, Cleveland, Philadelphia, Boston. There's no reason we can't begin improving right now. I certainly don't think we should simply call present methods to a halt and consider that in itself progress. All it is is an opportunity to begin to do things differently and better.

AUCHINCLOSS AND LYNCH: How important a role does the transportation mess play in the death of great cities?

JACOBS: It's very serious, but it's not the cause of our trouble. It wouldn't matter whether we had the automobile or not: the kind of wholesale planning we've been getting would still be very bad planning.

AUCHINCLOSS AND LYNCH: And the automobile is just an excuse for it?

JACOBS: Yes, one of the excuses, not a reason.

AUCHINCLOSS AND LYNCH: How about banning private cars from cities?

JACOBS: That's a pretty negative approach. I think people are pretty suspicious of schemes that offer them nothing for something. We should get rid of the automobiles, but in a positive way. What we need is more things that conflict with their needs—wider sidewalks, more space for trees, even double lines of trees on some sidewalks, dead ends not for foot traffic but for automobiles, more frequent places for people to cross streets, more traffic lights—they're an abomination to automobiles, but a boon to pedestrians. And then we should have more convenient public transportation.

AUCHINCLOSS AND LYNCH: Turn parking lots into skating rinks?

JACOBS: Yes. We constantly sacrifice all kinds of amenities for automobiles. I think we can wear down their number by sacrificing the roadbed to some of our other needs instead. It's a switch in values.

AUCHINCLOSS AND LYNCH: Do great cities, with all the noise and dirt and bad smells, seem livable places to you, really?

JACOBS: Parts of them are very livable, but these are by no means necessarily the most fashionable parts. Greenwich Village is livable, and the demand for city districts that are lively and interesting to live in and safe on the streets is much greater today than the supply.

AUCHINCLOSS AND LYNCH: Is it really possible to plan more areas in the image of Greenwich Village?

JACOBS: Of course you wouldn't want to reproduce the Village, but the same principles that work here can work other places, and do. The mixture of residential, commercial, cultural, and manufacturing buildings all in one neighborhood, the mixture of old and new buildings, the short blocks. In describing the neighborhood I live in in my book I was really describing a fairly ordinary sort of city place. Its values don't depend on a special kind of ethnic group or a high income. People from cities all over the country tell me that I was describing the kind of place where *they* live. I've been criticized for having a Bohemian or a working-class point of view. I don't know what class point of view I have, but it's city life I've been describing, and this is recognized by many, many people who live city lives. I think people who say that I am describing one peculiar kind of place—maybe it ought to be preserved, but it has nothing to do with cities in general—just haven't experienced city life at firsthand. And they aren't using their eyes.

AUCHINCLOSS AND LYNCH: How did you happen to pick this place to live?

JACOBS: An area may be dilapidated, as this was, but a certain person can sense its general social atmosphere, which may be hopeful and healthy. If it's a community, if it's stable, if people stay put, then you have a livable place. People ought to pay more attention to their instincts. There is an intuitive sense of what is right and comfortable and pleasant. When people talk to me about my book, so often they say, "I always felt that way about the housing project I live in, but I thought it was supposed to be good for us, and I never dared say it." When a lot of experts say one thing, then people stop trusting themselves. This is a mistake. After all, everybody who lives in the city can be an expert about cities.

AUCHINCLOSS AND LYNCH: What about city planners, the people who think they are the experts? How are they trained?

JACOBS: Quite a few are people who failed in architectural school and then went into schools of city planning. It's almost a sort of social-climbing profession. It attracts people who want to be in something that has the aura of being a profession and yet isn't awfully demanding to learn or practice. Every city has a planning department, in addition to all the housing and redevelopment agencies, and it's easy to get a job. You know, it's interesting—I get entirely different letters from architects and planners. Architects generally write me about the subject matter of my book, which is how cities work. Whether they agree or disagree, that's what they talk about. I haven't got a single letter from a planner yet that discusses the city; they talk about planning in the abstract. They are obsessed with professionalism. It's as if they were doctors who talked about doctoring and weren't at all interested in the human body.

AUCHINCLOSS AND LYNCH: How did the profession get started?

JACOBS: It started at a time when American cities didn't have planning commissions, and I think it attracted people who don't like to see what they are doing result in action. A whole body of dogma grew up, whole generations of teachers, who never put any of this into practice. It's an odd thing to prefer to be in the kind of enterprise where nothing happens. Then quite suddenly in the Thirties they began to get the opportunity to get results—not just what they wanted maybe, but, after all, these housing projects are *somebody's plans*.

AUCHINCLOSS AND LYNCH: Isn't one of the real troubles about city planning that they think so big?

JACOBS: Yes, this grandiosity is inherent in the orthodox planning dogma, and it's very simple-minded. You can't create the texture of a living city in one fell swoop that way. Things must grow. The kind of planning for a city that would really work would be a sort of informed, intelligent improvisation. which is what most of our planning in life is in any case. All plans—business, your children's education, whatever—are made like this, playing it by ear all along the way. Urban renewal, in particular, is a very peculiar form of planning. The whole notion of simultaneous uplift for an area has nothing to do with real life or growth. And then there is this ideal involved in it: that you should make things perfect and keep them that way. Well, this is a form of death, of course. Enormous sacrifices are made for city planning and almost all of them are considered a justification—a proof that if so many people or businesses are uprooted it *must* be progress. City planners are always saying you can't make an omelet without breaking eggs. But they are talking about people, not eggs! If planning helps people, they ought to be better off as a result, not worse off. There's this notion that certain groups of people must be sacrificed for the common good, but nobody quite defines what this common good is. Actually, of course, it is made up of a lot of smaller goods. It's not at odds with good for people in the concrete.

AUCHINCLOSS AND LYNCH: You've been criticized, just as you criticize the planners of garden cities, for assuming that favorable environment can determine values and ways of life. For you it's lively streets, for them trees and grass. But aren't you both physical determinists?

JACOBS: There's a distinction that I can explain best with an analogy. Suppose you are designing a room for a meeting. That's very different from determining what the meeting is going to decide. Society is an endless meeting, where people can be heard and seen and things can happen. But *what* the meeting decides is out of the hands of the designer except insofar as he is another member of society. The planners of garden cities had it all decided what the meeting should decide, what life should be like for people, what was and what wasn't good for them. This is true of all utopian thinking.

AUCHINCLOSS AND LYNCH: Well, the people who started the

French Revolution must have had an idea of how the meeting should turn out.

JACOBS: Oh, political action is absolutely concerned with how the meeting should come out. But it is quite a different kind of thing from physical design. And I believe that lively cities where society can operate in an intense way make meetings out of which very fertile and ingenious decisions can come. But if people are isolated, fragmented, if one income class is set off from other income classes, the meeting simply does not occur. If different kinds of talents don't come together, if different sorts of ideas don't rub up against one another, if the necessary money never comes in juxtaposition with the necessary vision, the meeting doesn't occur.

AUCHINCLOSS AND LYNCH: So meetings don't occur in suburbs?

JACOBS: Suburbs are perfectly valid places to want to live, but they are inherently parasitic, economically and socially, too, because they live off the answers found in cities. But I don't blame only the planners. By implication I blame everyone who knows in his bones that things are being done wrong and won't trust himself enough to act like the citizen of a self-governing country. We've had an awful abdication of the responsibility of citizens.

AUCHINCLOSS AND LYNCH: Isn't there something wrong with schools, that people should grow up with such a feeling of helplessness about the use of their own minds?

JACOBS: If I were running a school, I'd have one standing assignment that would begin in the first grade and go on all through school, every week: that each child should bring in something said by an authority—it could be by the teacher, or something they see in print, but something that they don't agree with—and refute it.

AUCHINCLOSS AND LYNCH: But perhaps people accept being pushed around by big plans because they have no access to their true feelings any more. Everything is so complicated today.

JACOBS: They *don't* really accept it. Part of the West End of Boston is being made over, and the Harvard Medical School and Massachusetts General Hospital have combined on a research project that looks into the mental-health aspects that go with urban renewal. One of their reports is called *Grieving for a Lost Neighborhood.* They say they have known for a long time from the way people feel about urban renewal at the time it happens to them that it is very disruptive and upsetting. And they go on to say that in spite of these previous findings, which they were ready to modify, they have been shocked to discover that the reaction of the majority must be described as *grief*—feelings of painful loss and longing that are sometimes overwhelming. And this is two years after they had been moved. You see, home is not just a building: it's a territory, the whole connection between you and other people and places. People *do* have feelings, they express them in every way they can, even while they are being ridden over roughshod. But they're intimidated by experts who tell them what they feel is selfish and ignorant, and unfortunately they are willing to believe it—to believe that there is even something disreputable about their grief.

AUCHINCLOSS AND LYNCH: The kind of apartments they build now, even the luxury ones, don't seem to work. People keep moving out in spite of the housing shortage.

JACOBS: That's how i got interested in this whole business. I wrote about projects before they were built, and they were going to be full of people strolling on the promenades and so forth and there were pictures of how delightful it all would be. But then I saw some of them built and they weren't being used that way. This struck me as interesting, and I tried to talk to the planners about it, but they weren't in the least interested. They just blamed the people. And it seemed strange that they weren't curious about what had gone wrong.

AUCHINCLOSS AND LYNCH: Did you talk to the people who lived in the projects?

JACOBS: Yes, a lot of them were there because their old homes had been, as they often put it, "thrown down." And of course there was it lot of resentment, which produces a fantastic turnover rate. The luxury buildings are essentially no different from the public housing projects. People don't like them. It's not a question of U or non-U—it's simply that people relate to the old-fashioned sort of apartment or brownstone better and will pay a premium for that reason. It isn't because they like broken-down things or that they have a sense of the past. It's simply that those are better places to live. And all this enormous planned building that's being done has accomplished little except to increase the housing shortage.

AUCHINCLOSS AND LYNCH: It's certainly made apartments unfit for human-type families.

JACOBS: Yes, but in New York it's also actually decreased the number of dwelling units. You have to consider how long the land lies unoccupied during demolition and building, too. If we would stop building *projects* and start building *buildings*, we could relieve the housing shortage much faster, with much less dislocation of people, without destruction of neighborhoods, and with increase of density where density needs to be increased.

AUCHINCLOSS AND LYNCH: What about the concept that nobody likes projects, but in terms of the American economy that's the only way it can be done?

JACOBS: Well, sure it's the only way it can be done if you contrive by every means to make it the only way it can be done. It is not done without great subsidies and immense powers of eminent domain. There's nothing spontaneous and inevitable about it. It took years to achieve, and it's based on the premise that cities are not good places. Take a human being. You know what a healthy human being looks like, but there have been periods in history when very unhealthy human beings were idealized. Chinese bound feet, for instance, or fashion models. But anybody whose children looked like that would worry.

AUCHINCLOSS AND LYNCH: How much do you think that fashionable architecture has to do with the disease of cities?

JACOBS: Architecture is in a very bad way today. It's getting a very mixed press and it's not just the Philistines who are rejecting it. It's novelists and artists and poets who are *most* rejecting of the kind of architecture we're getting now. The people are prophets, and architects should be very, very worried. They reply that they are being blamed for decisions that aren't theirs—for decisions that are built into the zoning or the legislation. But they have conspired in imprisoning themselves in these decisions, and they are not leading the way toward correcting them. They've begun to go nutty about novelty and very show-offish, vulgar things. And terribly egotistic. Largely because they don't know what else to do.

AUCHINCLOSS AND LYNCH: What do you mean?

JACOBS: If they had an esthetic based on function, on the way things work, they wouldn't have to fall back on nice effects, novelties, grotesque exaggerations. The Chase Manhattan Bank has ruined the skyline of lower Manhattan. This is an incredibly egotistic, insensitive thing for a building to do. And it's not just no-account architects who are doing these things.

AUCHINCLOSS AND LYNCH: Why this egotism? Have they nothing genuine to express?

JACOBS: It's partly lack of sufficient respect for function.

Function, which is supposed to be the basis of modern architecture, has almost unnoticed taken on a very different meaning from that had in the beginning. Then function meant the way a building was used. Frank Lloyd Wright revolutionized the home on this basis. Perkins and Will revolutionized the elementary school. Various buildings were really rethought in those terms. But now function has come to mean not the way the building is used but the function of the structure itself, the function of the material. So that architecture with a capital A has become more and more interested in itself and less and less interested in the world that uses it. Hence you get a term like *universal space*, meaning great, undifferentiated areas, that are really just an excuse for using dramatic trusses. In fact, such space works out very badly for almost any kind of use other than big auditoriums. In terms of function in the old sense one of the most "universal spaces" is an old brownstone house. Look at the different uses these can be put to: they are used as homes, shops, schools, offices, and none of these uses requires more than a minimum of change, because the combination of large and small rooms is remarkably adaptable. When architecture gets far away from interest in how it's used and in the world that uses it, and more interested in itself, then it's narcissistic. And like all things that get far from the truth it begins to have to be smart-aleck and say sensational things—about itself, because it has nothing else to talk about.

AUCHINCLOSS AND LYNCH: And instead of wanting to elevate people, architects just want to startle them?

JACOBS: Yes, and I must say architectural magazines have furthered this, largely because novel buildings make unusual and startling photographs. The enormous popularity of Mies and his façade architecture is, I think, largely owing to how well his buildings look in photographs.

AUCHINCLOSS AND LYNCH: What about Frank Lloyd Wright?

JACOBS: His buildings are hard to photograph. They always seem to me to look better and more exciting than they ever do in the photos. And for the same reasons he is never imitated successfully. Because architecture wasn't just a visual thing with him. He really rethought things in functional terms. This lack of attention to function today is not just a disease of architecture or city planning though. People no longer seem to know how things work. Idealized designs of many kinds ignore what objects do, or conceal what they do and how they do it. It's like locomotives we used to see, with their wheels and the whole business exposed. Then a skirt was put over them, concealing as much as possible. Much of what is called design today is cover-up.

AUCHINCLOSS AND LYNCH: Why?

JACOBS: I don't know. It's funny, we're supposed to be a country that's almost puritanical about work. Supposedly we do not think work is disgraceful. We almost glorify it. And yet we are very ambivalent about it. Mind you, I don't idealize the days before modern improvements. I think women's life must have been the most godawful drudgery. But I must say when I see old houses—I think we miss something today. The kitchens and laundries were so obviously for several people to work in together. We have an awful lot of lonely routine work now, and it isn't nearly so much fun as working in company. So we have to turn on the radio.

AUCHINCLOSS AND LYNCH: What do you think is the future of urban renewal?

JACOBS: I think it's dying of its own embarrassments and fiascos.

AUCHINCLOSS AND LYNCH: Has a balance sheet ever been drawn up of its successes and failures?

JACOBS: No, I don't think so. I was talking on television with a planner from upstate New York not long ago who was saying how grand and vital urban renewal is. And I said to him, "Name me one urban renewal project that is really successful." He thought a while and finally named a project that doesn't exist yet. It's just a plan. And I said. "No, the plans are always full of people doing just what you want, that's the thing about plans. Name me a project that's been built. A lot have been built by now." And he couldn't.

AUCHINCLOSS AND LYNCH: You seem to think city planners hate cities. Why do they?

JACOBS: I don't know. Lots of people hate cities, you know. But it's a very poor policy to try to prescribe to things you hate. Some of them do praise a lot of urban qualities of liveliness and diversity and contact among different kinds of people, but they really have no interest in how things work. They go on prescribing arbitrarily how things should be— how many people per acre, how much open space, and so on. This is wishful thinking. Like the plans where, because you provide a promenade, people are supposed to stroll on it. And because you build a shopping center, you think people will shop in it. No, I agree with C. P. Snow that it's terribly important to understand how things work, especially if you are going to tinker with them. Why do people use certain paths? Why are they here and not there? Why do stores succeed or fail economically? If you don't respect such things as that, you are just talking to thin air, just wishing.

HOW WESTWAY WILL DESTROY NEW YORK

INTERVIEW BY ROBERTA BRANDES GRATZ
EXPANDED FROM *NEW YORK*
FEBRUARY 6, 1978

Dorothy of Oz and anyone else born in Kansas would, no doubt, be dazzled by the sheer audacity of the plan. A real gold-brick road, $4,359 an inch, running 4.2 miles up the lower West Side of Manhattan, a six-lane tunnel built mainly on landfill from the Battery to 42nd Street, replacing piers up to 34th Street. The billion-dollar highway would likely replace a considerable part of the economy of lower Manhattan, including such things as the Gansevoort 14th Street meat market, employing 4,500 persons directly and responsible, in part, for another 3,500 jobs in nearby cafés, bars, restaurants, and markets that service meat-market employees. And the real-estate speculation and redevelopment fantasies of city planners, not to mention the construction disruption, would no doubt drive away even more business that survives on the Lower West Side only because of the lower rents there.

A decade of planned disruption that would create jobs in New Jersey, Pennsylvania, and Connecticut (but very few here in New York) and would leave in its wake the insular, inhospitable high-rise communities that urban planners love so much . . . Jane Jacobs, where are you now?

We found her in Toronto, Canada. America's foremost critic of mindless urban mast-planning had left the country.

Jane Jacobs is a member of a select literary group. Only once in a great while does a popular book have an impact so profound that conventional wisdom in a given area is perceptibly, permanently changed. Exceedingly small is the club of contemporary writers whose books—such as Nader's *Unsafe at Any Speed*, Galbraith's *The New Industrial State*, or Carson's *Silent Spring*—have dramatically changed the way we think about our society.

Jane Jacobs became a member of that chosen few upon publication, in 1961, of *The Death and Life of Great American Cities*. Before that book, urban renewal meant bulldozers and massive rebuilding, high-rise ghettos and four-lane highways. After its publication, much has happened: neighborhood rehabilitation, block associations, historic preservation on a broad scale, and a growing shift in population that is bringing the middle class back to the city center in restored neighborhoods like the West Village, SoHo, Park Slope, Columbus Avenue, and the North Shore of Staten Island. What Rachel Carson did for our neglected wilderness, Jane Jacobs accomplished for a growing urban wasteland.

Like Nader and Carson, Jane Jacobs was a soldier-philosopher who did not shy away from the battles her work soon provoked. She was a leader in the successful fights against the Lower Manhattan Expressway throughout the sixties, against the roadway planned through the center of Washington Square Park in 1955–56, and against the West Village Urban Renewal Plan in 1961. The expressway would have cut a wide swath through Little Italy and suffocated Chinatown with exhaust fumes. SoHo would have been killed before it was born.

So why has a woman who has fought so hard for New York neighborhoods left home and country? Jane Jacobs and her family were early "casualties" of the Vietnam War. Jacobs lived thirty years in this town, married here, and raised three

children here. In 1968, however, her two almost draft-age
sons, James and Edward, made the decision to resist. As she
always had, Jane Jacobs put family first and went to Canada.

The Jacobs family found refuge in Toronto, now Canada's biggest city. To their delight, they discovered a town
"much like New York used to be." In the past ten years, Jacobs
has kept a low profile, scrupulously avoiding the public spot-
light, refusing constant requests for interviews and speaking
engagements. However, she continues to be an active critic of
urban master-planners, even in Toronto, and is now working
on another book.

Late last month, I talked with Jane Jacobs in her Toronto
home. The subject was Westway, and it brought an immediate and emotional response: "Westway is second only to
bankruptcy in its importance to the city," said Jacobs. "It is
the single most important decision New York is facing about
the future. No mayor will make the difference to New York
that this highway will make. If Koch does nothing more than
kill Westway, he'll be one of the great mayors of the city."
Westway, continued Jacobs, is a metaphor for the city; how
one feels about it depends on one's vision of what the city is
and what it can become.

●   ●   ●

GRATZ: How did you get involved with the Lower Manhattan
Expressway fight?

JACOBS: There was so little in the newspapers that I wouldn't
have been aware that it was going on if I hadn't run into

people in City Hall. That's how badly it was being covered. It wasn't really regarded as news.

Father LaMountain [of the Church of the Most Holy Crucifix, in Little Italy] and his parishioners had been fighting it. It would have wiped out his street, church, parishioners, shops, and more. This was right after our West Village fight, and we'd won it, so he asked me if I would come to a meeting on this in early '62. I was reluctant. I had put in a horrendous year. We didn't get the West Village Urban Renewal designation removed until February '62. It was a whole year. I'd hardly had any sleep, it seemed to me, in that whole year. We hardly even had any meals to ourselves because everybody was dropping in. But that was all right. It was necessary.

There were meetings going on all the time. People were dropping in to find out what was the news. We had an arrangement with the neighborhood. We would leave our front light off if we didn't want anybody to come in, but if the light was on, they could come. Most of the time, everybody was at work. Only in the evening could we do these things, so that's the kind of year the whole family had. And we wouldn't have missed it—I mean, we'd all love to have missed having the problem, but as long as we had it, we wouldn't have missed fighting and winning it. No question about that. But we were pretty tired, and the idea of another fight . . . it took some persuasiveness on the part of Father LaMountain to have me just come to the meeting.

I began to understand that this fight was connected to the fight over Washington Square. If this expressway came through, our victory in Washington Square would have been a very pyrrhic one indeed. The ramps would be coming off, and if they didn't come off through Washington Square, they'd come off damn close—and in other places in the Village, too. These monsters come back, you know.

Also, some of the things that we hadn't understood at all about the Urban Renewal fight began to become clear to me. We kept hearing about a map that was in David Rockefeller's Lower Manhattan Development Office. Various people who had seen it would tell us about it. It showed combinations of highways and new real estate developments on both sides of Manhattan, all the way up the West Side. So I began to see that these were other facets of the very same fight, that somebody had a great vision of how New York was to be. We kept running into this vision, and it was a monstrous vision. You would see this piece of it and that piece of it, and it wasn't paranoid to think that it was an overall plan that the public really didn't know that much about. It was clear what a disaster it would portend for the Village and other neighborhoods.

GRATZ: It seems like a conflict right out of *Death and Life*.

JACOBS: Right. And it was even much worse than I had ever believed or dreamed when I was writing the book. I couldn't believe there would've been this much stupidity about New York.

GRATZ: Tell me about your arrest in 1968.

JACOBS: The state was holding a hearing to focus on a big promotion for all this great land development that was going to occur. All of a sudden, they were soft-pedaling—or ignoring—the number of cars, because they were now worried about the pollution factor. A committee was researching the expressway's pollution impact, and they were very frightened. People tried asking: if it wasn't going to increase the pollution because there would not be many new cars, how could the cost be justified? And they would say: that's not what this hearing is about. It was a great charade.

A very curious thing was occurring. I was used to hearings at the Board of Estimate, where the microphone for the speaker faces the people holding the hearing—the ones going to make the decision. The speaker's back was always to the audience. At this hearing, however, the microphone was directed the other way. The speaker's back was to the officials. This was very symbolic.

So when it was my turn to speak, I drew attention to this—how we weren't talking to the hearing officers, we were just talking to each other. It was a charade. Furthermore, it wouldn't matter if we were talking to these officials, because they were not the people who made the decisions anyway. They were just errand boys, sent from Albany to preside while we let off steam under the guise of a hearing. It was phony as a hearing.

I decided that at least I would send them back to Albany with the message that we really didn't like this, and since talk would never amount to that kind of a message—since they didn't hear anything—I planned to just walk across the stage and let them know that I was not content to remain down there talking to my fellow citizens, that I wanted to give them an immediate message. And I said, "Anybody who wants to come with me, come along." I addressed them instead of the hearing officers. They had set it up for us to talk to each other, so I was going to do that. And so I started up the stage. And pretty nearly all the audience got up and began to follow me as I walked across the stage. That's all I was going to do—walk across the stage and down the other steps.

And this threw them into the most incredible tizzy, the idea of unarmed, perfectly gentle human beings just coming up and getting in close contact with them. You never saw people so frightened. They had a policeman up there on the stage. As I came up on the stage with, I guess, pretty nearly all the audience coming along, too, everything was quiet, absolutely quiet, except the chairman, a state engineer, kept yelling, "Officer, arrest this woman! Arrest this woman!"

He didn't arrest me at first. He came over to me and he said, "Mrs. Jacobs, come on over here and sit down." And so I sat down where he suggested, and the chairman was now standing blocking the way. Nobody knew what to do. The woman with the stenotype had jumped up in alarm, and her tape was all running out, and she grabbed her stenotype. So people began picking up this tape that was all around now and sort of tossing it around. That was all that was happening: this eerie silence and sort of leisurely kind of confetti. It was really surrealistic, because nobody was tearing it up or doing anything violent, just wafting this paper. And the engineer was yelling, "Arrest this woman! Arrest this woman!" Everybody else was absolutely silent. Nobody knew what to do.

The policeman said, "March down the other side; just make a gesture." So, I made some derogatory remark to him about these people holding the hearing. I forget what I said; it was pretty plain. Something like, "They've got their minds made up; they're just trying to do us in, these people." And he said, "Aren't they, though." And so there I sat.

This scene went on, and after a while I thought, "Somebody has to bring this to an end. Nobody knows what to do any more than I do." So I got up from the chair—all these frightened men went down the other side—and went to the microphone again. I said, "What's the charge? Why am I being arrested?"

The policeman said, "It's at the request of Mr. Toth [John Toth, chief engineer for State Department of Transportation]. I wouldn't arrest you except that he has demanded your arrest."

So, I said again, "What are the charges?" And he said, "Well, that will be worked out at the station house. But I must arrest you, I'm sorry."

And I said, "Well I think they're making a mistake."

And he said, "I think they are too, but I have no choice."

He was really nice. He was always on my side. I was booked on disorderly conduct. A court date was set. When we got to court I waited and waited all morning. My case wasn't called. My arresting officer came down to me at one point and said, "They're making new charges against you. They're opening up law books they've never opened up before."

The charges they came up with were riot, inciting to riot, criminal mischief and obstructing government administration. Four years in jail. They'd have liked to put me in for it too. They really would.

They made out what a dangerous character I was: inciting to riot. I was a menace on the streets. I had to be silenced. If I spoke I was to be put right in jail, because it would probably be incitement to riot.

GRATZ: What happened next?

JACOBS: At the pre-trial hearing, they turned up with all kinds of lies about how I had damaged the steno-type machine. That's what the "criminal mischief" was. Mr. Toth was there, and he gave a horrendous account of how terrifying all this was. I guess it was, to him. I guess he wasn't putting this on, but it sounded ludicrous to me. But he really was terrified.

I had a very expensive, top-grade lawyer, and we had to hold fundraisers to pay him. The lawyer's strategy was this: to put it off and put it off, as long as possible, until they cooled down. Because they were furious and they wanted to really sock it to me. He found that out.

By the time it came to court, we plea bargained. I pled guilty. I was convicted of disorderly conduct and let off with a suspended sentence and ordered to pay for the damage done to the machine. I hadn't done any damage to the machine. They had said a whole lot about how it had had to be repaired and how much it had cost, hundreds of dollars' worth of damage to this valuable machine. This was all made up, a hoax. But that was all they had to really substantiate anything—except my standing around where I wasn't invited.

What we wanted to do was get a receipt and then investigate and see what corruption and phoniness there was about this receipt, since we knew the machine had not been damaged. The lawyer got no answer at all about the receipt, so then I wrote to the judge, saying that I had this judgment to pay. I didn't like this debt hanging over my head. I enclosed a copy of the letter that had been sent, told him about the phone calls, and asked him to please order them to comply with their part of the court order, so I could comply with my part. Got no answer. But at least I had the letter on the record, if ever it was said, "Well, she was ordered to do this and she didn't." I guess they could see the trap that we were hoping they would fall into. We would have had a field day if they had tried to falsify a repair bill.

GRATZ: Did the arrest accomplish anything tangible?

JACOBS: Some issues you fight with lawsuits and buy time that way. With others, you buy time by throwing other kinds of monkey wrenches in. You have to buy time in all these fights. The lawsuit way is more expensive.

We did accomplish something with all this mess. The Feds held a hearing, declaring the expressway environmentally unacceptable. Well, well, that verdict *really* changed the subject. My arrest bought some time, and it was well worth it. That's why I plea bargained, to buy more time. I would have gone to jail if necessary. But the only point of it was to buy time to continue working in Washington on the environment and get a judgment against the expressway.

GRATZ: How did the fight end?

JACOBS: It was a little like the West Village fight. After a while, Washington wanted the West Village thing to end. It was giving the urban renewal program a bad name all over the country. There were editorials in the *Saturday Evening Post* about the West Village. There were pictures all over the U.S. of people protesting it with adhesive tape and Xs on their glasses. It was a bad image for them, bad press that they were getting. I think highway people in Washington began to feel the same thing was happening with the expressway, too.

It was one of the earliest cases to go this way. And it was an unequivocal thing. You could see how much pollution would occur. The state had used these increased car figures very early to justify spending this much money and doing this amount of destruction because of how much traffic it would accommodate. But now it was over, and, eventually, demapped.

• • •

GRATZ: How can one oppose Westway when the city so desperately needs jobs to revitalize the economy?

JACOBS: That's the question asked again and again by the parade of highway advocates at public hearings. But they never tell us who will get those jobs. And they never count the jobs that may be lost in the displacement process that inevitably accompanies new development.

A trade-in of the Westway money, for transit rehabilitation plus a modest rebuilding of the West Side Highway, according to a six-month Sierra Club study, would deliver 103,000 man-years of employment, both inside and outside of New York City; Westway promises only 78,000, and most of those will be outside the region—in plants manufacturing the steel, cement, and other component parts and materials. What's more, most of the promised Westway jobs are temporary; but many permanent jobs are endangered by the displacement of businesses along the Westway construction site.

For too long, New York has cannibalized itself for the sake of temporary construction jobs; meanwhile, we lose all sorts of low-cost industrial space and drive out all kinds of existing jobs. During the Lower Manhattan Expressway fight in the sixties, I asked Harry Van Arsdale, head of the Central Labor Council, how he felt about all the jobs that would be wiped out. He said to me, "Oh, I can't be concerned about those kinds of jobs." He was only interested in the construction jobs. To this day, that's the highway lobby's job argument, even for Westway.

GRATZ: A project like Westway, if it's well designed, can enhance the urban environment, in addition to promising redevelopment of a blighted port of Manhattan.

JACOBS: Plenty of expressways have been put into areas—or proposed for areas—where they will not uproot people, or where displacement is minimal. And it still does enormous damage to a city. And it's still the wrong priority for the money.

This is a wrong way to treat transportation in the city. And it's an uneconomic way, and it's a polluting way, and it's got internal contradictions that cannot be justified. And it's a national problem. We're writing about a specific one, but it doesn't mean that if you can, in another city, find an expressway that actually doesn't uproot anybody and doesn't cut off the waterfront, yet cuts through the city, that it's okay. It's not.

GRATZ: Isn't there a reactionary tenor to Westway's opposition?

JACOBS: Quite the opposite. Westway is only one small piece of a plan for an overwhelming highway network for Manhattan that would, piece by piece, Los Angeles–ize New York. It's an old plan that dates back to 1929. Just think of that. New York prides itself on being up-to-date, and it's being run by a half-century-old plan. What we have are pieces of this plan that keep surfacing every few years. Nobody would ever consent to the insanity of doing the whole thing, and yet piece by piece it gets done.

Robert Moses was a master at this technique. He would build a bridge without saying there must be a highway at either end. Or he'd build a road and say nothing about a great big bridge that would be needed. It was a piecemeal approach and the people would have had a fit if they had seen the whole thing and what it implied.

GRATZ: That sounds a bit hysterical. After all, we're talking about a highway on landfill that goes from the Battery to 42nd Street—not paving over all of Manhattan.

JACOBS: Take a look at the 1929 plan and you'll feel differently. The plan includes not just the West Side Highway but a ring around the entire shoreline of the island, more like a big U, actually, because the top doesn't connect. Then it calls for lacings—highways running through the middle of the island from east to west to connect the sides of the ring.

GRATZ: But this master plan was never put into effect.

JACOBS: A good deal of it was. But the worst could still come if the roadway system gets bigger, more ramps are added, and the crosstown lacings appear. The FDR Drive is part of the plan, as is the West Side Highway. You don't see the crosstown highways because we fought them all over the last twenty years. The Lower Manhattan Expressway, set to run across Broome Street, was one of the lacings.

That expressway proposal was preceded by a great deal of propaganda against the area we now call SoHo. It was called Hell's Hundred Acres or the Valley then, in the mid-fifties. It would be a good thing, so the argument went, to run a highway through there and get rid of these horrible buildings and turn it all into something like Washington Square Village—sterile new high rises.

Killing the expressway bought a marvelous piece of New York. SoHo was already reviving—at least starting to, and what has become SoHo would have been wiped out. Chinatown and Little Italy would have been devastated, too. So our three oldest, most prized Lower Manhattan neighborhoods would have been lost.

GRATZ: So what has the long-defunct expressway plan to do with Westway?

JACOBS: If Westway goes in, the Lower Manhattan Expressway will be revived. It probably won't be on Broome Street now. Canal, mentioned in the 1929 plan, and always considered an alternative route, is more likely. A draft report prepared for the Highways Department last April refers to a "Canal/Delancey Street Corridor"—the expressway in a modified form. And that would create pressure to rebuild the rest of the West Side Highway north of Westway to interstate standards, enlarging its carrying capacity and cutting into Riverside Park. And there would be new crosstown traffic routes like 34th Street and so on up the island. Westway will never be an isolated highway segment. It's like a tree trunk that has to grow branches.

GRATZ: Why are you opposed to a highway system in Manhattan whose basic intent is to remove traffic from our hopelessly congested streets?

JACOBS: It's nonsense to say that this net is going to remove traffic from the city's streets. It's got to have its ramps to draw traffic onto and off city streets, until the system has invaded the entire city, disrupted its very fabric.

As long as the highway scheme focuses on the outside edges, things stay calm. The minute the arterial roads feeding the system appear, it scares the hell out of people. Only at that point does it become clear how the master-planners will destroy the city as we know it, destroy the whole fabric, turn it over to traffic. There are plenty of people who don't want a city like this, either because of the direct harm it would do to their home, or where they work, or the air they breathe, but also because of the inhumanness of that sort of environment. It fills them with horror, repels them, runs contrary their vision of what the city should be.

Those people don't want Manhattan turned into Los

Angeles, a city that's built for automobiles and not for people. They don't want a city that would destroy its SoHos, Chinatowns, Little Italys. Plans like the expressway or Westway are death sentences for neighborhoods. Before the first building falls, the plan enforces deterioration, stops investment in existing businesses. Businesses leave when they see the handwriting on the wall, or don't even try to establish themselves in such a location. Property owners hold out for the lucrative buyout. It's a miracle when a place like the North End in Boston or the West Village keeps on improving, and people keep putting money in when a death sentence hangs over it. They can only do it with the courage of knowing that they aren't going to allow that death sentence. Or being totally ignorant that it exists.

But the bankers are never ignorant about it and stop giving loans. When there's a death sentence like that on an area, you always have to work around it and get odd bits of money and so forth, which can make a very good area in the end, if it's done.

GRATZ: But the decay and devastation on the West Side today started long before Westway was proposed.

JACOBS: There was a reason those piers on the West Side were left to decay and a reason why the shipping was withdrawn from them and taken over to Port Elizabeth and other places. This area had a different destiny in store for it. It was going to be a great real-estate ripoff when its time came. Public and private investment went elsewhere.

GRATZ: But what do you do for trucks, which are necessary for the city's economic life and compete with cars for road space?

JACOBS: The best way to improve truck access is to take out all the passenger cars you can, and transport people by mass transit. This relieves truck congestion, speeds up traffic, saves money, and makes a better climate for industry in New York.

• • •

GRATZ: A pro–West Side Highway, anti-Westway position will be hard to sell.

JACOBS: We don't have it nearly as tough as the other side. Westway proponents have a terrible dilemma. Their position is based on an enormous contradiction. If they say Westway is going to accommodate a lot of additional traffic in the years to come, they run into the problem of air pollution, even if the increased traffic moves around and through the city somewhat faster. If the increase in traffic is just 2 percent each year for the next twenty, it will be horrifying in terms of additional pollution in the city. So advocates of Westway have to minimize for argument's sake the increase in traffic and its implications.

On the other hand, these highways cost so much, how are they going to justify spending $1.16 billion if Westway won't carry more traffic than is currently handled by existing roadways? Something so enormously expensive must provide the public with some commensurate enormous service, or the whole thing is pointless. Which is, in fact, the case. Westway will do an enormous *disservice* to the city by generating

increased traffic that brings horrendous environmental damage. Westway advocates must prove it would do more than accommodate the same traffic that a rebuilt West Side Highway
would take care of. And a West Side rehab at $38 million is a
long way from a $1.2-billion Westway.

If the environmental damage is minimized, the cost can't
be justified. But both issues are never examined at the same
time, at the same hearing.

GRATZ: The added bonus of Westway is the new housing and
parks that will be added, with through traffic out of the way,
underground.

JACOBS: That's the same carrot the expressway advocates
used in the sixties. The battle for the Lower Manhattan Expressway started in the late fifties, but a few years later people
were more sensitive to environmental damage. So the whole
argument for the highway changed to the subject of new land
development. Suddenly it was a wonderful plan for new housing, parks, fountains, and reconstruction that would grow
up on both sides of the expressway. A whole new piece of the
city to develop.

Westway is the same scam. The grandiose land-
development scheme is a red herring created to sell the project. Instead of talking about the highway, proponents keep
trying to talk about the landfill and what will be built on it,
and they hope that nobody asks the questions: "All right, if
the landfill and parks and apartment houses are so great and
the city really will have money to run these parks and the
people of New York really do have enough income to fill up

this many more apartments and so on, then why not do it on its own? Would you promote this landfill plan without the highway? Would it be totally unfeasible without the highway? Why? What is wrong with this scheme without the highway?" The reason it is so great *with* the highway is because it is simply meant to sell the highway.

GRATZ: You seem to feel that the landfill scheme is a myth. But the head of the design and planning phases of Westway, Lowell Bridwell, won federal approval of a new principle: Federal money for interstate highways in cities should include the extra cost of putting the highway underground, minimizing its obtrusiveness and providing free space to the city—for parks, etc.

JACOBS: The landfill proposal, though the planners never emphasize this, is nothing more than empty land and some zoning changes. It's up to the city to go beyond landscaping and build the parks from its own funds. Then private developers will pick up the tab for housing.

The city can always use more parks. But why are we letting the parks we have go to hell? If there's not enough money for those that now exist, how will there be any for new ones? Or will we let the old ones deteriorate further while we spend money on new ones in the way Robert Moses put money into highways and let mass transit fall apart? Why are we adding new land to the city when some proponents of Westway agree with "planned shrinkage" in areas like the South Bronx, where sewer and utility lines and streets already are in place? There's no sense to any of it.

If there ever was a real-estate scheme set up to fail, it's the Westway development. Don't forget the Battery Park experience. All we'll get is more mud flats. By the time the land scheme is a failure, nobody will care because the highway will be built.

GRATZ: So who is for this project if it makes no sense?

JACOBS: All the same people, influence peddlers, who always get a hearing no matter how discredited their advice has been in the past. President Carter told Congressman Ted Weiss that he was in favor of Westway because David Rockefeller assured him that it would be good for the city's economy. That's what Rockefeller said about the World Trade Center and look what at a disaster that's been for the real-estate market.

GRATZ: What will be the future of the West Side if Westway is stopped?

JACOBS: By fighting the expressway, we were accused of wanting to burn up the city because these buildings were dilapidated firetraps. Well, they were firetraps because they had all sorts of inflammable stuff in them that would make Rockefeller Center a firetrap. And the fire laws were not being enforced. It was an area that was to go.

Revitalization of the West Side would be easy compared to SoHo. It's already starting in so many places. The West Village is spilling out to the Hudson at Greenwich and Washington streets, where warehouses are being converted to apartments and co-ops.

The West Side waterfront could turn into a success story, as in Toronto, Seattle, Boston, or Vancouver. In Boston, people used to live on the piers and there were lots of restaurants on them. In the thirties, the piers were an amazing place to visit. As soon as city planning in Boston began to be taken very seriously, these things were scheduled for demolition. Suddenly they were "ramshackle." Now, of course, they're being rebuilt, coming back. Old industrial buildings there are being converted into housing, shops, and restaurants. Some of the piers themselves have actually been reconstructed.

This is one of the things New York could learn. Think of the things the unused piers could be used for. Look at the location and the pilings already there. They could build new mixed-use areas—commercial, residential, parks, artist housing—right out overlooking the river. It's happening naturally, and it could be encouraged, the way SoHo was allowed to happen. And it would finance itself.

Plenty of room exists for fill-ins. Lots of vacant space that certainly ought to be built on before you add new land at enormous expense, if that's ever necessary. And the new land wouldn't be a success until these fill-ins were done in any case. But we must kill Westway first. It's nothing but a $1.16-billion manicure that will take away the area's innate charm and keep it under dust and dirt for twenty years at a minimum.

•   •   •

GRATZ: What are the prospects for stopping the Westway? What do the opponents have to do?

JACOBS: The public has been going through a great learning process in the last couple of decades of how to defeat the highway men. And in response, the highway people—naturally—have worked up other defenses. The environmental impact and air pollution thing was a new weapon for the public. The changing of the subject was a defense move for proponents. Now there is a requirement for public participation. The public demanded it, and got it. In earlier highway schemes, there was no such requirement. So, the defensive weapons are the new ways of manipulating the public and of using public relations to give the impression of public participation. With Westway, they've anticipated a lot of the troubles that they had with the Lower Manhattan Expressway fight. And this time, it's a harder fight because they know that they can't give up on Westway and start with another piece of the net.

GRATZ: If we stop Westway and recoup some of that money, what should we spend the money on?

JACOBS: Transit. It's no accident that the transit system has continued to go down while enormous amounts of money have been spent on highways. There's not unlimited money to spend on transportation. It will be the ruination of New York if you keep trying to supply, first and foremost, roads for the automobile and let everything else just fit into the margins.

GRATZ: Isn't it hard to say no to new roads and new ways to accommodate automobiles? People seem very accepting of this as the norm.

JACOBS: Not really. It's running the other way. Time is on our side. There's more doubt about these things. The fights get harder and harder, more and more widespread. In 1955 and '56, it was unheard of to fight a thing like the roadway through Washington Square, unheard of to talk in the kind of terms that educated people now find it perfectly natural to talk in. At the time, the terms were: *which alternative do you prefer, the road through the park, or the widening of the road around it?* Most people at the time just couldn't imagine any other alternative.

And it was Edith Lyons and Shirley Hays—who sat in the park with their little kids—they wondered why they should be stuck with either of these, and why you had to have additional roads for traffic around Washington Square at all. And they were considered crazy women who just didn't understand the facts of life. Isn't this just like a woman to think that way?

GRATZ: You're opposed to the automobile, aren't you?

JACOBS: I'm not a fanatic against automobiles. In fact, I think it's a very good thing we have them instead of horses. I'm not a fanatic at all. Furthermore, I don't think they need to be eliminated from cities by any means. I don't think we should bar them.

But the minute you start whittling away the other amenities, the minute you begin devoting virtually all the transportation money to this one purpose, then you're eroding the city.

GRATZ: But you wish car lovers would stay outside the city limits?

JACOBS: There are some people who prefer to travel by automobile—no matter what. They love what Marshall McLuhan calls the "one-ton metal cocoon." Okay. No one is making them get out of their cars if they want to be in them. But they have to accept some of the disadvantages of travel by car in the city. They make their own choice. But the point is that the city should not be remodeled for cars.

It's impossible to remake large cities to accommodate all the cars or potential cars. And if you try, you have to distort priorities and that's what erosion is all about. That's why the stakes are higher in the Westway fight.

If Westway were built, it would be a very clear signal that there was no hope for the future of New York, that it could do nothing but repeat expensive, disastrous mistakes. That it couldn't turn itself around, and that it would be okay to keep building new highways or expanding existing ones. Other cities will follow.

They just keep obsessively repeating the same mistakes. This is what's absolutely frightening about Westway: that there's no way New York can turn itself around. The Lower Manhattan Expressway was preliminary. The chips are down on this one and herein lies the future of New York.

GODMOTHER OF THE AMERICAN CITY

INTERVIEW BY JAMES HOWARD KUNSTLER
EXPANDED FROM *METROPOLIS*
MARCH 2001

Toronto always gives me the strange sensation of being in a parallel universe, one in which I might be in a great American city—say, Detroit, St. Louis, or Cleveland—if only we had not gone through the cultural convulsions of the postwar era and tossed our cities into the dumpster of history. Hollywood constantly uses Toronto as a set for Anycity, USA, but the truth is that it is in much better shape than almost any American city.

In Toronto you see office buildings every bit as hideous and grandiose as in America—and the same overly broad streets, poorly furnished with medians, trees, and other urban decor considered impediments to express motoring. But despite these shortcomings, Toronto is alive. Its downtown streets are teeming with people who actually live in the city center in apartment buildings and houses, and the sidewalks are jammed until late at night. The public realm, where the buildings meet the sidewalk, is active. Toronto is what many American cities wish they could be.

Jane Jacobs—the renowned urbanist and author of *The Death and Life of Great American Cities, Cities and the Wealth of Nations, The Economy of Cities, Systems of Survival,* and other books—lives here. Her house is in the Annex neighborhood on a serene residential street off Bloor, the main drag of the University of Toronto, which in that vicinity resembles the Eighth Street shopping district of Greenwich Village—where

Jacobs so famously lived and wrote years ago. There are boutiques and bistros alongside copy shops, Asian groceries, and shoe-repair joints. Jacobs's home is a Toronto "double," a type of semi-detached brick row house, with a generous neoclassical white wooden porch, a Dutch-style gable end, and ivy growing up the wall.

Jacobs lives here alone now; her architect husband, Robert, passed away in 1996. One son and his family live right down the block, and see her often. The eighty-four-year-old author was a little incapacitated from hip surgery when I stopped by last year. The inside of her house was pure sixties Bohemian Intellectual. The Jacobses had removed some interior walls, so the first-floor kitchen, dining room, and living room all flowed together. There was a great groaning wall of books, of course, and other surfaces were still painted the bright colors of the go-go era, when the family moved there. A breastplate made from beach bones, shells, and pieces of driftwood was displayed near the bay window in front; the tablecloth in the dining room was a bold East Indian print. There were drawings by Jacobs's daughter, who lives in the backwoods of British Columbia, and lots of family photographs everywhere. Her office is a spare bedroom upstairs in the rear, where it is especially quiet.

Jacobs still looks like that famous photo of her taken in the White Horse Tavern in the West Village more than three decades ago (a cigarette in one hand and a beer mug in the other). Her hair is the same silvery helmet with bangs, and her big eyeglasses emphasize her role as the ever-penetrating observer, with an impish overlay. She still likes to drink beer, and worked on a bottle of some dark local brew while we talked.

During the course of our conversation we were seated at her dining room table.

• • •

KUNSTLER: What was it like for you coming to New York for the first time?

JACOBS: The first time I was ever in New York I was twelve years old. Let's see, I was born in 1916, so that would have been 1928, and it was before the crash. And I went with the parents of some friends, and I guess we drove there. I guess the car was left in New Jersey. Anyway, we got over on a ferry and we landed in downtown Manhattan. And I was flabbergasted at all the people in the streets. It was lunchtime in Wall Street in 1928 and that was . . . the city was just jumping. It was all full of people.

KUNSTLER: What year did you come there to live full-time?

JACOBS: That was, let's see, '34.

KUNSTLER: And what was your impression then? Was it a different . . .

JACOBS: Yes, it was different. Because it was the difference between the high tide of the twenties' prosperity, and depression.

KUNSTLER: Was it palpable—could you really feel it and see it?

JACOBS: I could see contrasts, even from that first visit. Especially downtown. There were a lot more unemployed people in '34, and there weren't any in '28.

KUNSTLER: Where did you find yourself going when you got to New York in the twenties? Did you just naturally find your way into Greenwich Village, or did you start elsewhere?

JACOBS: My sister was already there. She was six years older than I was.

KUNSTLER: What was she doing?

JACOBS: She had studied interior design in Philadelphia, and so she came to New York hoping to get a job as a designer. But she couldn't in the Depression. She got a job in a department store—Abraham and Strauss in Brooklyn, in the home furnishings department. That was the nearest thing she could get to her line. So I came along, and she had been living on East 94th Street. Imagine, she and several other girls, they lived in this house. It was a rooming house. It was very cheap rent. This is a very expensive area now.

KUNSTLER: Yeah, but the Jacob Rupert Brewery was up there until 1957. I lived on 93rd Street for a while myself. You would go through these brewing cycles when the neighborhood would be full of this smell of beer and hops.

JACOBS: She moved to Brooklyn, Brooklyn Heights, to a house that is not there anymore. It was a six-story walk-up, and we lived on the top floor. It was a nice neighborhood, though. It was near the St. George Hotel. It was before the highways went in there. So I would go looking for a job every morning. I would look in the newspaper and see what seemed likely and which employment agencies were advertising. I would usually walk over the Brooklyn Bridge into Manhattan. And then, after I was turned down for all these jobs, I would spend the rest of the day looking around where I had ended up. Or if I had ended up in a place where I had already looked around I would spend a nickel on the subway and go arbitrarily to some other stop and look around there. So I was roaming the city in the afternoons and applying for jobs in the morning.

And one day I found myself in a neighborhood I just liked so much . . . it was one of those times I had put a nickel in and just invested something. And where did I get out? I just liked the sound of the name: Christopher Street. So I got out at Christopher Street, and I was enchanted with this neighborhood, and walked around it all afternoon and then I rushed back to Brooklyn. And I said, "Betty I found out where we have to live." And she said, "Where is it?" And I said, "I don't know, but you get in the subway and you get out at a place called Christopher Street." So we went to look for a place where you got out of the subway at Christopher Street.

KUNSTLER: What did you find?

JACOBS: We found an apartment on Martin Street. I had a job by then, I guess we didn't go looking immediately. And one of those mornings I hit the jackpot and got a job.

KUNSTLER: And what was it?

JACOBS: It was in a candy manufacturing company as a secretary.

KUNSTLER: So you did a bit of secretarial stuff.

JACOBS: Oh, I did secretarial work for about five years.

KUNSTLER: Did you have any inkling that you were going to be a professional intellectual?

JACOBS: No, but I did have an inkling that I was going to be a writer. That was my intention.

KUNSTLER: Did you hang out with any of the Greenwich Village bohemians of the day?

JACOBS: No.

KUNSTLER: Did you see them around?

JACOBS: Yes, I guess I did. But I didn't have any money to hang out in bars. We were living very close to the bone. In fact there were considerable times when Betty and I were living on Pablum because my father was a doctor, and he told us that the most important thing was to keep our health and that we should not skimp on nourishing food. So when we didn't even have any money for nourishing food, we knew that Pablum for babies was full of nourishment, and we also knew that bananas were good—and milk. And so that's what we would live on until we got a little more money. It was a powder that you mixed up, and it was not good.

KUNSTLER: Sounds a little grim.

JACOBS: Yeah, but we had a good time, and we didn't go for long periods on this, and we did keep our health, and it was nourishing food.

KUNSTLER: Yeah, in the sense that astronauts eat stuff out of tubes.

JACOBS: That's right. I don't want to give you the impression that we lived for long periods like this. Maybe toward the end of the week . . .

KUNSTLER: Tell me how you found yourself venturing into the life of a public intellectual.

JACOBS: I began writing articles right away. And this combined with my afternoons I had spent looking at different areas of the city, and I wrote a series of articles that *Vogue* bought about different areas of the city. The fur district—you see, they had something to do with the kinds of things that the readers of *Vogue* were presumably interested in—although

I didn't know who I was writing these for when I wrote them. But then I saw what I was doing, and I tried this.

KUNSTLER: It must have been exciting to sell magazine articles.

JACOBS: It was. I got $40 a piece for them.

KUNSTLER: That was a lot of money then.

JACOBS: A lot of money! Because at the job I had, I got twelve dollars a week. Of course I didn't sell many of these. I wrote about the fur district, the flower district, the leather district—let me see—the diamond district, which was down on the Bowery then. So I was trying to be a writer all the time. And eventually, not right away, but later on, I got to write Sunday feature stories for the *Herald Tribune*. But I didn't get paid as well for those. But then I wrote a few things for *Q Magazine*—oh, about manhole covers, how you could tell what was running underneath you by reading what was on the manhole covers.

KUNSTLER: You hadn't gone to college, by the way.

JACOBS: I hadn't wanted to go to school after I finished high school. I was so glad to get out.

KUNSTLER: Were you a troublemaker?

JACOBS: Yes.

KUNSTLER: I sympathize—I didn't like school either.

JACOBS: I would break paper bags in the lunch room and make explosions, and I would be sent to the principal, and that kind of thing. I was not really a troublesome person. I was not really destructive in any way, but I was mischievous.

KUNSTLER: Were you a comedian?

JACOBS: Sort of, yeah.

KUNSTLER: Naturally, I was reviewing some of your books the last couple of weeks. They stand up so beautifully. One would have to suppose at the time that you wrote *The Death and Life of Great American Cities* that you were pretty ticked off at American culture. For instance you wrote, "It may be that we have become so feckless as a people that we no longer care how things do work, but only what kind of quick, easy outer impression they give." And you wrote that around 1960, or the late fifties.

JACOBS: Yeah, I began in 1958 and finished it in 1960.

KUNSTLER: It seems to me that American life has changed very little in that regard. In fact, I actually go around on the lecture circuit telling audiences that we are a wicked people who deserved to be punished . . . and I am not religious. So what was your state of mind? Were you ticked off at American culture? Was it the culture of civic design? Was it Robert Moses? Was it some combination of those things? Was it the

Bauhaus? What was it that was getting under your skin in those days?

JACOBS: What was getting immediately under my skin was this mad spree of deceptions and vandalism and waste that was called urban renewal. And the way it had been adopted like a fad and people were so mindless about it—and so dishonest about what was being done. That's what ticked me off, because I was working for an architectural magazine, and I saw all this firsthand, and I saw how the most awful things were being excused.

KUNSTLER: You must have already been acquainted with things like Corbusier's "Radiant City," and some of the schemes from the twenties, and the Bauhaus. By this time, Gropius had become installed at Harvard and Mies Van der Rohe . . .

JACOBS: I didn't have any feeling about these one way or another. It was just another way of building. I didn't have any ideology, in short. When I wrote "we have become so feckless as a people," I had no ideology.

KUNSTLER: But you were angry.

JACOBS: But I was angry at what was happening and at what I could see firsthand was happening. It all came to me firsthand. I didn't have any abstractions about American culture. In the meantime, I had gone to Columbia a couple years, but I hadn't been taking classes in American culture. I sat in on

one in sociology for a while, and I thought it was so dumb.
But I had a wonderful time with various science courses and
other things that I took there. And I have always been grateful
for what I learned in those couple of years.

But I'll tell you something that had been worrying me:
I liked to visit museums that showed old-time machines, and
tools and so forth. There was one of these museums in Fred-
ricksburg, Virginia, which was my father's hometown. I was
very struck with the way these old machines were painted.
They were painted in a way to show you how they worked. Ev-
idently, the makers of them and the users of them cared about
how these things were put together and how what moved
what, so that other people would be interested in them.

I used to like to go to the railroad station in Scranton
and watch the locomotives. I got a big bang out of seeing the
locomotives and those pistons that moved the wheels. And
that interested me: how they were moved by those things and
then the connection of that with the steam inside, and so on.
In the meantime, along had come these locomotives that had
skirts on them, and you couldn't see how the wheels moved,
and that disturbed me. And it was supposed to be for reasons
of aerodynamics, but that didn't make sense. And I began to
notice how everything was being covered up, and I thought
that was kind of sick.

KUNSTLER: So the streamlining of the thirties bugged you?

JACOBS: That's right. So I remember very well what was in
my mind [when I wrote] "that we have become so feckless as
a people." It was those skirts on the locomotives that I was

thinking about, and how this had been extended—we didn't care how our cities worked anymore. We didn't care to show where the entrances were in buildings and things like that. That's all I meant. It was not some enormous comment on abstract American society. And I thought, this is a real decadence of some sort.

KUNSTLER: Well, apropos of the slums, we now know after the fact that slum clearance and urban renewal was a disaster. And, you know, I am a big critic of urban renewal. But it's been a big problem with American cities that they are not places people could really care about that much.

JACOBS: That's not altogether true. There were lots of areas in American cities that people cared about very much. And you can tell that by the fights they had when they were being put out of them. One of the things that angered me so much with urban renewal was the West End of Boston. There's a phantom community to this day. They have a newspaper that comes out periodically, these displaced people and their children. In '58, I talked to two architects who helped justify the destruction of the West End. And one of them told me that he had had to go on his hands and knees with a photographer through utility crawl spaces so that they could get pictures of sufficient dark and noisome spaces to justify that this was a slum—how horrendous it was. That was real dishonesty.

The other was greatly respected, a well-known architect who could give his opinion that this area should go. And he told me that on the whole, those buildings were so well constructed that they were undoubtedly better than anything that would ever be erected in their place. He also said that some of the buildings were just so beautifully detailed that it was heartbreaking that they must be wrecked. And both of these architects knew better, but supported the destruction of that area.

KUNSTLER: But isn't that the whole tale of the mid-twentieth century? That scores and scores of architects and planning officials went along with something that was really pernicious?

JACOBS: That's right. And they did it dishonestly. And how could they justify that? I would argue with them about these things, and they could justify it because urban renewal was a greater good, so they would bear false witness for this greater good. Why was this a greater good? Everybody knew it was, because slums are bad. "But this isn't a slum." "Oh well." They didn't care how things worked anymore. That was part of what was making me so angry. Also, they didn't seem to care what part truth and untruths had in these things.

KUNSTLER: Of course, there were a lot of people involved, and not all of them were mendacious. A lot of them seemed to be just idealistic, but it is hard to understand how that degree of misplaced idealism could sweep through a whole generation.

JACOBS: I don't understand that myself. I don't understand how these changes [happen]. McCarthyism was an example. The fear that that it struck into people. How could all these people turn into such sheep so suddenly? And when this miasma of McCarthyism lifted, it was almost as magical.

We were trying to get signatures on a petition that a [freeway] wouldn't go through Washington Square. This was in the fifties, and we set up a table with petitions near the park and asked everybody who came by and was enjoying the park if they would sign. And so many people wouldn't sign. We'd say, "Well, you don't want a road through here, do you?" No, they didn't want a road through there, but "You don't know who else might be signing. It might be dangerous to sign." Sometimes, a husband would tell a wife. So that's when this strange fear pervaded everything. But I remember when it lifted, we were fighting a battle to save a neighborhood at that time. This was one of the neighborhoods that I lived in that was designated a slum and had all the same kind of faults brought against it.

KUNSTLER: Was this the West Village?

JACOBS: Yeah, it was no slum. Loads of the places that were destroyed weren't slums.

KUNSTLER: Who wanted to knock down West Village?

JACOBS: It was the Rockefellers wanted to knock it down. But that's never been established—watch out, you might be gotten for libel. But that was really where it was generated, in the Downtown Lower Manhattan Association, which was David Rockefeller's organization. And they wanted it.

There were all these essentially private visions of how beautiful the city would be, and it was to be all these high-rises.

And there would be a little enclave, and all the most expensive and pretty houses in the village would be left. But all the parts along the edges—the ones that people of lower income occupied—especially of mixed uses . . . that was our sin in the West Village. We had all these mixed uses. And now all these former manufacturing places are turned into the most expensive lofts with condominiums that sell for over a million dollars. These people, even as real estate experts, they didn't know from nothing. They were so ignorant. Not only about what they were destroying, but about what people would like.

I am digressing. I still get angry about it.

KUNSTLER: What's your level of indignation these days?

JACOBS: I still get angry. We've got a prime minister who seems to be intent on destroying our health system and education system. But I have gotten a thicker skin. I can get angry about these things without feeling like vomiting, if you know what I mean.

KUNSTLER: Did you ever meet Robert Moses?

JACOBS: No, I saw him only once, at a hearing about the road through Washington Square, which was to be an entrance ramp to the Lower Manhattan Expressway. He was there briefly to speak his piece. But nobody was told that at the time. None of us had spoken yet because they always had the officials speak first, and then they would go away, and they wouldn't listen to the people. Anyway, he stood up there gripping the railing, and he was furious at the effrontery of this, and I guess he could already see that his plan was in danger. Because he was saying "There is nobody against this—*nobody, nobody, nobody,* but a bunch of, a bunch of *mothers!*" And then he stomped out.

KUNSTLER: Did he do more damage to New York than Albert Speer did to Berlin?

JACOBS: I haven't been to Berlin. I don't think that we have to compare them. He did an awful lot of damage to New York, yes he did. And I think that New York is just healing itself now. But to go back a minute about these strange hysterias that sweep the people wholesale, I also remember just when McCarthyism lifted, as I saw it in a concrete way—firsthand. It was when we were fighting to save our neighborhood in the 1960s. You see this way of making people scared to sign petitions and everything.

The Citizens Housing and Planning Council had all the settlement house people. A lot of them had also become idealists who didn't know what they were doing. The head of it held a press conference, and he came out with a blast about these terrible, selfish, awful people who were trying to stop this wonderful clean-up urban renewal scheme in Greenwich Village. And he called us not only selfish, but he called us pinkos. And that would have scared a lot of people. But it was just not an ideological battle at all. It was a battle for a neighborhood. It had all kinds of people.

And one of the people—someone said he had been a communist in the thirties, actually a communist, with a party card! And he was a very good guy. He was an artist, and he thought up lots of our best visual schemes, and so we had a meeting: what are we going to do about this? And the consensus was, it doesn't matter. This has nothing to do with warfare. This is saving our neighborhood, and it doesn't matter, and we don't care. So as soon as somebody said that, that struck everybody. Of course, that was the only sensible thing to do. Then a couple of days later, there comes this thing in the *Times* about how we're pinkos. And everybody laughed. And we all memorized the list of terrible characteristics that we had. Those were just my firsthand, concrete bits of knowledge that this hysteria had passed. Why did it pass? Why could people suddenly laugh at that?

• • •

KUNSTLER: You were born in Scranton, Pennsylvania, and you spent really the prime of your life living in Manhattan— in Greenwich Village specifically.

JACOBS: Well, I wouldn't say that.

KUNSTLER: No?

JACOBS: [*chuckles*] I'm still in the prime of my life.

KUNSTLER: You spent a certain portion of your life in New York City. Why did you move to Canada?

JACOBS: Well, we came in protest of the Vietnam War. We had two draft-age sons. They wouldn't have been exempt. One of them was a physicist. He had graduated from college and had been accepted in graduate studies in physics. And this was a time when the U.S. was very scared about Sputnik—he would have been exempt. The other one might not have been. They would have preferred to go to jail than to go to war. And my husband said, "You know, we didn't raise these boys to go to jail." And in any case we didn't like the war. We sympathized with their antagonism to it. And so we decided to come to another country. We are just not cut out to be citizens of an empire. And we liked it here, and our children liked it here.

KUNSTLER: Did you at first not intend not to stay forever?

JACOBS: We didn't.

KUNSTLER: It must have been very disruptive.

JACOBS: It would have been disruptive if we had thought of ourselves as exiles. People who think of themselves as exiles, I find, can never really put their lives together. We thought of ourselves as immigrants. And it was an adventure, and we were all together.

KUNSTLER: But you were leaving quite a lot behind.

JACOBS: Yes, we were but this was another thing that we found out when we got here: Americans don't really think that other places are as real as America. We were leaving things behind but we were coming to other things that were just as real and just as interesting and just as exciting. And people would ask me after we had decided to stay, "Well, when are you coming back?" "Well, we're not. We are living here." "Oh, but you can't just—you've got to come back to real life." And I would say, "It's just as real." This is very hard for Americans to understand, and I think that may be the biggest difference between Americans and people elsewhere. Canadians know that there are places just as real as Canada. It's a self-centeredness that's a very strange thing.

KUNSTLER: Is there something dangerously or weirdly smug and complacent about Americans?

JACOBS: Yes, they have got it so dinged into them that they are the most fortunate people on Earth and that the rest of the world—the sooner it copies what America is like, the better. I still have a lot of family in America. I still have a lot of friends there. There is a lot that I admire there very much. When I find America getting criticized too much outside America, I want to tell them how many things are good about it. So I am not a hate-America person. I really came here for positive reasons. We stayed for positive reasons, because we liked it. Why did I become a Canadian citizen? Not because I was rejecting being a U.S. citizen. When I became a Canadian citizen, you couldn't be a dual citizen. Now you can. So I had to be one or the other. But the reason I became a Canadian citizen was because it simply seemed so abnormal to me not to be able to vote.

KUNSTLER: Did any of your American friends object to this move?

JACOBS: They just thought it was like I was going into a dream land, or a wonderland or something. Nobody in my family did. Nobody among my close friends. They might have thought it was a little odd because it didn't occur to them.

KUNSTLER: Whom did you consider your professional or intellectual colleagues in the sixties and seventies? Any figures that we would think of? I'm just throwing names at the wall—Dwight Macdonald, Norman Podhoretz? Who did you hang out with?

JACOBS: I liked my editor and still do—my editor and publisher Jason Epstein. I knew Dwight MacDonald, but very slightly. I liked him.

KUNSTLER: So you didn't have a particular coterie?

JACOBS: No. In *The Death and Life of Great American Cities*, I have a whole list of people who I acknowledge receiving help from, but it's not intellectual help

KUNSTLER: Were there any of your contemporaries who were writers on urbanism whom you admired?

JACOBS: I admired some of the people who I worked with at *Architecture Forum*. And William H. ["Holly"] Whyte. He was a friend of mine. He was an important person to me, and he was somebody whose ideas . . . yes, we were on the same wavelength. And it was through Holly that I met Jason, and he became my publisher. He had started Anchor Books, which were the first trade paperbacks. Holly introduced me to him. I told him what I wanted to write, and he agreed to publish it and give me a contract.

KUNSTLER: How many years did it take you to compose *The Death and Life of Great American Cities*?

JACOBS: Well, not very long. I started it in the fall of '58, and I finished it in January of '61. So it was two years and a few months. But I had been thinking about it for a long time. And although I didn't know what I was gathering information for, I was gathering information for it.

KUNSTLER: Many of the dogmas of modernist city design, which we both deplore in our books, were believed in by people who were not stupid. To what extent do you suppose that even intelligent people are captives of their time or place? How do we account for the tenacity of terrible ideas such as Corbusier's Radiant City—especially among the mandarins of the elite graduate schools that train our cultural leaders?

JACOBS: I think that intelligent people, to a great extent, are captives of their time or place.

KUNSTLER: Is it as simple as that?

JACOBS: There are always mavericks among them. Now we are going to have to get into the education system.

KUNSTLER: Well, you know the people at the elite universities today at Harvard and Columbia and Yale are extremely hostile to the kind of ideas that you were retailing forty years ago, and which some of my colleagues are still trying to persuade the American people would be good ideas. And they are extremely hostile to the New Urbanist movement.

JACOBS: Yes, I know they are.

KUNSTLER: In a way that seems almost pathological. How do you explain that? Are they just defending indefensible doctrines? What is it that they are trying to protect?

JACOBS: They are trying to protect their worldview. Everybody's got a worldview, whether they know they have it or they don't. They might even get it when they are little kids. Suppose they get it when they are in college, which is often the case, or in high school—whatever. Everything they learn after that, or everything they see after that, they fit it into that worldview. And they are making coherence of what's good, what's bad, what will work, what won't work, what's noble, what's ignoble, and so on . . . all through this filter.

KUNSTLER: Well, we would have to be guilty of that, too.

JACOBS: Yes we all have this. But there are two ways you encounter things in the world that are different. One is that everything that comes in reinforces what you already believe and everything that you know. The other thing is that you stay flexible enough or curious enough and maybe unsure of yourself enough—or maybe you are *more* sure of yourself,

I don't know which it is—that the new things that come in keep reforming your world view.

The same when you're writing a book. By the end of the book, it is quite different from the way you thought it would be when you started it—both in form and what it contains and what you think. Well, you tipped in a lot and you digested a lot—it wasn't pre-digested in your view. And it changed what you thought and how you see things. And a lot of these people, they learn something, and they are so sure of it, and it's a terrible threat to them. I don't think it's so much of an intellectual threat, but an emotional threat: their whole worldview will have to go through that upsetting thing of being confused.

KUNSTLER: Let me give you an example of something I recently encountered in Canada. I was on a panel at the Royal Architectural Institute of Canada, and it was my turn to say something, and having walked around Ottawa that morning and observed that so many of the new buildings presented blank walls to the street, I made the observation that it would probably be a good idea if Canadian architects recognized that buildings should have a bottom, a middle, and a top. And that the bottom should maybe behave differently than the middle. And these people freaked out. And started saying, "Goddamn you, we are not classicists, don't try to pawn off classicism on us. We are beyond that." And I thought this was really extreme.

JACOBS: It's emotional.

KUNSTLER: I said, "I'm not asking you to be classicists. You can do it in Aztec modern or you can do it in retro–George Jetson. You can do it any way you want. But to recognize that a building has a top, a middle, and a bottom is not a style issue." But they didn't want to hear it at all. And they were full of indignation.

JACOBS: It threatened them.

KUNSTLER: But here's the thing. Why do they want to keep on producing buildings that are killing their cities—buildings that people hate? What possible motive could they have for wanting to continue doing that?

JACOBS: They don't think that they are killing cities. They don't think that people hate them. Everything they have taken in says this is enhancing the city. Doesn't that tell you something? It tells you that their own image of themselves was being threatened by what you were saying. And it was *not* their ideas of buildings—it was *not* their ideas of the cities. It has to do with themselves and their image of themselves.

KUNSTLER: Here is another example. Corbusier comes up with a cockamamie scheme for destroying the Right Bank in Paris, the Marais District. And the idea immigrates to America, and it takes America by storm. Meanwhile, in France, every year, Corbusier goes back to the officials in Paris and says "I have this wonderful idea to destroy the Right Bank." And they laugh at him. For years—decade after decade—they laugh at him. They never do what he proposes. They do build a lot of crappy stuff outside of the center of Paris. But they never knock down the center of Paris. In America, we took that idea and we just loved it. Why didn't we laugh at it?

JACOBS: Lots of people did.

KUNSTLER: Not enough to prevent it from happening.

JACOBS: That's true. Well, it was prevented in Greenwich Village. And in the end that whole thing petered out.

KUNSTLER: Ed Logue, who passed away earlier this year, was kind of an exemplary figure of his time. He was a product of Yale, of the elite universities, and he went on to inadvertently destroy both New Haven and much of central Boston by directing modernist urban renewal campaigns in the 1960s. Did you watch these schemes unfold, and what did you think of them?

JACOBS: I thought they were awful. And I thought he was a very destructive man, and I came to that opinion during the first time I met him, which was in New Haven. He was telling me all the wonderful things he was doing and was going to do.

KUNSTLER: Do you remember the circumstances when you met him?

JACOBS: It was when I had started working on my book. I went to see him to find out what was happening in New Haven and so on. And he did tell me some useful things. In particular he told me one very interesting thing. He said the best thing that could happen to San Francisco would be another earthquake and a fire. Like the one that happened in 1904. And I was appalled at this. I had been to San Francisco, and I thought it was wonderful place. He was serious about it—he thought that all that should be wiped out and built new. Boy, in my books, he went down as a maniac.

KUNSTLER: Well, New Haven never recovered. He gutted a large part of downtown, put a mall there that has never been successful—and which I think may be either completely or partly demolished now. He put in a convention center that has also been a bomb and drove the freeways through. And in Boston, he was responsible for the City Hall Plaza. He and Henry Cobb and I. M. Pei. It seems to me that Boston City Hall Plaza has been a failure from the very beginning.

JACOBS: Oh, of course it was. But he didn't get to destroy the North End—which he intended to do. He had even sent in the application to the urban renewal people.

KUNSTLER: I lived in Boston in 1972, and I remember the North End as being a tremendously vibrant place. It was also very blue-collar. No yuppies had moved in at all. It was an Italian neighborhood, very insular, but tremendously active—full of all the pork stores, the cheese stores, and the cookie stores. But what do you remember about Logue's campaign in Boston?

JACOBS: Well, I can tell you why Ed Logue was valued. The editors of my magazine, of *Architectural Forum*, believed in all this urban renewal stuff. And I saw who their heroes were— and Ed Logue was one of their heroes.

KUNSTLER: Did this aggravate you?

JACOBS: Sure, but I used to argue with them about these things. And I didn't bring them around to my way of thinking. They wanted to live in an exciting new world. That's what they wanted. Some of the things you wrote about in your book—about people who had their greatest adventure in war time—I think that vision of an exciting new world that they will create and inhabit gave them some purpose in life.

KUNSTLER: Did you see the General Motors Futurama exhibit at the 1939 fair?

JACOBS: Yes.

KUNSTLER: What was your feeling at the time, if you remember it?

JACOBS: Oh, I thought it was so cute. It was like watching an electric train display somewhere, you know? It was just very cute.

KUNSTLER: Did you have an inkling that this was going to turn out to be Dallas in 1985?

JACOBS: No, of course not.

KUNSTLER: Did you think it was a fantasy? That it wouldn't happen?

JACOBS: Yes, I thought it was like those cute electric trains. It was a toy.

KUNSTLER: You've lived through most of the twentieth century, and it must make for a dizzying view of contemporary history. For instance, you've seen pretty much the whole rise of the automobile from its days of stupendous promise before World War II, to its utter savaging of the American landscape and townscape. Can you tell us how your own view of the automobile and its consequences evolved, and if your view changed over the decades of your life?

JACOBS: My family had an automobile before I was even born. My father was a doctor, and he needed an automobile to get around. A generation earlier, it would have been a horse and buggy. This automobile was a tool of my father's, just as much as the bag he carried. We never thought of it as an all-purpose conveyance. For instance, if we wanted to go to downtown, which was two miles from where we lived in Scranton, we went down to the corner and got the streetcar. We were never chauffeured to things. When my father's office hours started to coincide with one of my brothers and me being in high school very close to where he worked, we used to ride down with him. And once in a while our family would take a trip. I remember when I was four years old, going to Virginia in the car to visit his relatives. Oh, and I saw how the White House lawn was cropped in those days—there were sheep on the lawn.

KUNSTLER: Was there a point when you began to sense that the automobile might be sort of a pernicious thing?

JACOBS: I didn't see the automobile as a pernicious thing. I saw what was happening to the roads as a pernicious thing—the widening of roads and the cutting down of trees. And then later on, of course, knocking down buildings—existing buildings. It was the roads I saw as being the destroyers. Perhaps that is a foolish distinction to make. The automobiles weren't running into the houses and knocking them down, the automobiles weren't cutting down the trees and so forth. Again, I'm not an abstract thinker, as you can see. The immediate concrete thing was what the roads were doing.

KUNSTLER: Well, here is a concrete thing. We have a railroad system that even the Bulgarians would be ashamed of.

JACOBS: Yes, and we in Canada do, too. It used to be a wonderful system.

● ● ●

KUNSTLER: You've said that it is much nicer to live in a city where things are getting better, not worse. I agree with you because I live in a city, Saratoga, that has gotten a lot better just in the last twenty-four months. We have gotten more main street buildings built in the last thirty-six months than in the entire twentieth century. Ones that are worth a damn, that are not one-story cinder block bunkers. And it's a remarkable thing. So what's going on in Toronto?

JACOBS: Our downtown keeps getting better all the time. Even the sidewalks are being widened here and there. You can hardly find a gas station anymore. Buildings have been put in, and often very nice buildings. And there's lots of people living downtown now. That was a distinct policy of the city. We had a remarkable mayor, whose name was Barbara Hall. She went to work to get the zoning and the whole vision of this changed and believe me, it was very hard for her to educate her planning department to be able to accept this or do this. The various visions she had were excellent.

KUNSTLER: How did she whip all these guys into shape?

JACOBS: She just talked endlessly to anybody that might be involved, and she educated them and got them around to this view. It took a lot of work and a lot of talking and a lot of belief in what she was doing.

KUNSTLER: Toronto has a remarkable quality for a North American city—it's alive. Have you visited any cities in the heartland recently—such as Detroit, St. Louis, Columbus, Indianapolis—and seen their desolation? I find them absolutely heartbreaking. The small towns are destroyed, too, by the way. Detroit went from being something like the fourth wealthiest city in the world to a complete wasteland in less than fifty years. What are your thoughts on what happened to American cities?

JACOBS: It's a tragedy, and a totally unnecessary tragedy.

KUNSTLER: The destruction continues.

JACOBS: Yes, because nothing has really changed. Talk has changed, but regulations haven't changed, lending systems for these things haven't changed. The notion—and I tell you, this even extends into New Urbanism—the notion of the shopping center as a valid kind of downtown. That's taken over. It's very hard for architects of this generation even to think in terms of a downtown or a center that is owned by all different people, with different ideas.

KUNSTLER: We are starting to return to that particularly in the work of Victor Dover and Joe Kohl.

JACOBS: I don't know them.

KUNSTLER: They are young guys who were trained at the University of Miami by Duany and Plater-Zyberk, and they started their own firm about ten years ago. They have done two projects where they have taken dead malls and imposed a street and block plan over them and created codes so that the individual lots could be developed as buildings, not just as a megaproject. I think that's definitely the direction the New Urbanists are going in. I think that we are leaving the age of the megaproject.

JACOBS: Here's what I think is happening. I look at what happened at the end of Victorianism. Modernism really started with people getting infatuated with the idea of "it's the twentieth century, is this suitable for the twentieth century?" This happened before the First World War, and it wasn't just the soldiers. You can see it happening if you read the Bloomsbury biographies. That was one of the first places where it was happening. But it was a reaction, to a great extent, against Victorianism. There was so much that was repressive and stuffy. Victorian buildings were associated with it, and they were regarded as very ugly. Even when they weren't ugly, people made them ugly. They were painted hideously.

KUNSTLER: I can see how things like Richardsonian buildings—you know, those heavy, red sandstone buildings—could scare people. But we look at them today, and all we think about is, "God, you could never find masons that skilled who could do that kind of work." It seems unbelievable. It seems superhuman.

JACOBS: Yes, but it was oppressive—especially the Victorian house. And lots of them weren't oppressive in themselves. They were often very airy and gingerbready and fancy. But they were associated with all this stuffiness.

KUNSTLER: Well the family was sort of institutional. You couldn't go out and buy Velveeta. If you wanted cake, you had to bake a cake. Or have a cook do it. This period fascinates me, by the way, this period just before and after the First World War. What I keep coming back to is the idea that it represents a kind of nervous breakdown for Western civilization. You have this tremendous hope going into the twentieth century of a golden age to come, and then it was shattered.

JACOBS: Did it ever shatter! There was the League of Nations, and oh, it was going to be such a brave new world.

KUNSTLER: You were particularly harsh on Ebenezer Howard and Patrick Geddes and the Garden City movement of the early twentieth century. It was, in some ways, another one of those really bad ideas that a lot of intelligent people fell for— including Mumford, who got sucked in really big.

JACOBS: Oh yes.

KUNSTLER: It seems to me that both a cause and a symptom of our predicament is this near-total confusion in American culture now about what is the city and what is the country. What's rural and what's urban. It's all one big mishmash to us, and we are not able to design for it.

JACOBS: What was a really major bad idea about the Garden City was: you take a clean slate and you make a new world. That's basically artificial. There is no new world that you make without the old world. And Mumford fell for that, and the whole "this is the twentieth century" thing. The notion that you could discard the old world and now make a new one. This is what was so bad about Modernism.

KUNSTLER: Did you know Mumford, by the way?

JACOBS: Yes.

KUNSTLER: Were you friendly or were you adversaries?

JACOBS: As far as I was concerned, we were friendly. It was very funny. He was furious at *The Death and Life of Great*

American Cities, absolutely furious. He thought—I never gave him any reason to think this—he thought that I was a protégée of his, a disciple. I think because he thought that all younger people who were friendly were his disciples.

KUNSTLER: And he thought that you had turned on him?

JACOBS: I think that's what he thought. He was kind. I first met him when I gave a talk at Harvard in 1956. I was substituting for my boss, who had to be away in Mexico. And I had awful stage fright. I had resolved that I would never make a speech because it was so painful to me. And I was informed at the office that I had to make this talk—this ten-minute talk at Harvard. And I told them that I wouldn't do it. And the managing editor said I had to. So I said, "All right, I'll do it—only provided I can do what I want."

So I made a talk and I made an attack on [urban renewal]. Mumford was in the audience. It was a real ordeal for me. I have no memory of giving it. I just went into some hypnosis and said this thing I had memorized. And I sat down, and it was a big hit because nobody had heard anybody saying these things before, apparently. And this is why Holly Whyte got me to write that article for *The Exploding Metropolis*, because of this speech. Anyway, Mumford was in the audience, and he very enthusiastically welcomed me. I had hypnotized myself, but I had apparently hypnotized them too. But I believed what I was saying.

KUNSTLER: But then a few years later, Mumford attacked you?

JACOBS: I met him some more times and everything was amiable. I had my doubts about him because we rode into the city together in a car. And I watched how he acted as soon as he began to get into the city. He had been talking and all pleasant, but as soon as he began to get into the city, he got grim, withdrawn, and distressed. And it was just so clear that he just hated the city and hated being in it. And I was thinking, you know, this is the most interesting part.

KUNSTLER: I have a feeling that the Manhattan of his middle age—and perhaps even of your youth—was in some ways a tremendously overwhelming kind of place. It had never been seen before—New York was this giant oppressive machine. I grew up in it myself. There is something about New York that is despotically mechanistic—it's not all like Greenwich Village. Whatever his quarrels were with you, I do regard him as just being a marvelous writer, so crisp and lucid.

JACOBS: He was a very good writer, and you know, he had lots of good ideas.

KUNSTLER: But he was also captive to that turn-of-the-century idea that density and congestion are the enemy of cities.

JACOBS: Thin down the cities and disperse them over the countryside. Sure. And your question about how intelligent people are creatures of their time and place—it is absolutely true, and he was very much formed by his time and place—and so were we all.

KUNSTLER: He wrote about the Victorian era as the "brown decade." That might have been Edith Wharton or Henry James's term, but it was obviously a dark image.

JACOBS: You can get an idea of how oppressive it seemed. There was a generation or two that felt this very strongly. The whole center of their world view was a reaction against Victorianism and everything associated with it. They were absolutely ruthless with it.

KUNSTLER: Urbanism per se is in still in complete discredit in the United States. The only solution that we tend to bring to our failures of urbanism are what I refer to as nature Band-Aids—the landscaping fantasias, the bark mulch, the juniper beds intended to hide the blank walls of post-modern buildings, the berms, the buffers, and all the rest of the tricks from the landscaping industry. In a way, it seems to me that this comes from the Garden City idea—that somewhere in the early twentieth century, we decided that the city just wasn't any good and that we basically had to replace it with the country.

JACOBS: No, there were loads of people who didn't reject the cities. My parents were delighted to live in the city. My mother came from a small town and my father came from a farm. They thought the cities were far superior places to live, and they told us why. And there were all kinds of people who believed that.

KUNSTLER: It's self-evident that American cities are for the most part abandoned, vacant, not cared for, and in a state of decrepitude in many cases.

JACOBS: That's right. That's what a city means to most Americans.

KUNSTLER: I am going to St. Louis tomorrow. St. Louis is the proverbial doughnut hole.

JACOBS: Absolutely. Which happened on purpose. Practically their whole downtown was wiped away, and they put that arch up. They decided that their whole business section was a slum.

• • •

KUNSTLER: I'd like to turn to economics, which is another principal area of your interest and I think perhaps one that is underemphasized in your career. I'm also interested in systems theories, but particularly the ones that address the great blunders of civilization. It seems to me that the American living arrangement, the "the fiasco of suburbia," as Léon Krier calls it, is approaching a kind of tipping point beyond which it might be difficult to carry on. I have a theory that we don't have to run out of gasoline in order to throw places like Houston, Phoenix, San Jose, Miami, and Atlanta into terrible trouble. All that's necessary is a mild to moderate chronic instability in the world oil markets. It seems to me that we are sleepwalking into an economic and political trainwreck.

JACOBS: I know things won't go on as they are now. People who try to predict the future by extrapolating in a line of more of what exists—they are always wrong. I am not saying how it is going to go. But it is not going to go the same. This is a continuation of what I was actually saying about the revolt against Victorianism. Here comes a generation or two that just can't stand what the previous generations did. And for whatever reasons, they want to expunge it. And they are absolutely ruthless with the remnants of it. But I don't think of it as an economic or political trainwreck. I think of it as one of these great generational upheavals that's coming. And I think that part of the growing popularity of the New Urbanism is not simply because it is so rational, and not simply because people care so much about community (or even understand it), or the relation of sprawl to the ruination of the natural world. They just don't like what is around. And they will be ruthless with it.

KUNSTLER: I wonder if it will take an economic shock to prompt the majority of American to really reconsider their living arrangements.

JACOBS: I don't think it's that rational, the idea that this is unsustainable. I don't think that's the reason. Suddenly, they can't stand what the generations before did. There was no reason for Victorianism to be reacted against in those terms.

KUNSTLER: You were a little harsh on the City Beautiful movement in *Death and Life*, although personally, I look back on it and I see the sheer artifacts that they produced as being just awesome. Some of the best apartment buildings in New York City. The best single-family houses in America were produced during the American Renaissance. Just the sheer excellence of what they left behind is kind of stunning.

JACOBS: Yes, but it also had that weight of authority that people were reacting against. So I think that things are going to change just because people get too damn bored with what they have.

KUNSTLER: You say that you are not theoretical or abstract. As a practical matter, there is something called the Hubbert Curve, the petroleum depletion curve that says that we will reach a peak of world oil production and then we will go down the slippery slope of having less and less oil, having oil that is harder to extract, or oil that is less economical to extract. And of course, this is happening in different regions and different parts of the world. The two places in the world that basically saved our asses in the last twenty years were the north slope of Alaska and the North Sea oil fields. They are scheduled to reach peak production in the next year or so. After which their production will decline. And after that most of the oil in the world will be produced by people who hate us. How does that work for us economically?

JACOBS: Well, you see, all my life I have been hearing that the oil was going to run out. It never happens. They keep discovering new oil fields. The world is apparently floating in oil fields.

KUNSTLER: Well, it's possible that my proposition is a fallacy. But what if it's not?

JACOBS: I basically don't think that the way we do things is that dependent on one resource, such as oil. There can be different kinds of engines for cars. I think that solar heating and wind heating can substitute for a lot of uses for oil. I'd like to see those things happen because they are more sustainable in any case. But I do not think that running out of oil is going to bother us that much. I think we have got to be rescued by something, or we really are going down a slippery slope.

KUNSTLER: If it's not petroleum, then what is it that is putting us in peril?

JACOBS: I don't think it's any one thing. Nothing is so clear in history that is it happens for any one [reason]. It seems that a lot of things come together to make great changes. And I think that one of the things in this case is a reaction against Modernism and everything associated with it.

KUNSTLER: But we are stuck with all this stuff?

JACOBS: Yes, now that's the next thing. I do not think that we are to be saved by new developments done to New Urbanist principles. That's all of the good and I am very glad that New Urbanists are educating America. I think that when this takes hold and when enough of the old regulations can be gotten out of the way—which is what is holding things up—there is going to be some great period of infilling. And a lot of that will be makeshift and messy, and it won't measure up to New Urbanist ideas of design—but it will measure up to a lot of their other philosophy. And in fact if there isn't a lot of this popular and make-shift infilling, the suburbs will never get corrected. It's only going to happen that way. And I think that it will happen that way.

KUNSTLER: I have the greatest admiration for the New Urbanists. The hardest work for them to do is the urban infill.

JACOBS: But what nobody is even thinking about now is the suburban infill.

KUNSTLER: I think that a large percentage of the residential suburbs are going to be the slums of the future. Some of them will be rescued. Some of them won't be. In your book *Cities and the Wealth of Nations*, you focused on the "master economic process" called "import-replacing." The idea that a city and its region would only prosper if, over time, it started to furnish for itself many of the goods or services that it formerly imported. For instance, the rise of the U.S. as a great commercial nation in the late nineteenth century was a direct result of our cities starting to make the tools and machines and finished goods that we formerly got from Europe. With the latest model of the so-called global economy, we are given to believe that import replacement is no longer significant. To the extraordinary degree that an overwhelming majority of the products sold in the U.S. are made elsewhere. Is this a dangerous situation?

JACOBS: [*chuckles*] I think that it's a more dangerous situation. The standardization of what is being produced or reproduced everywhere: where you can see it in the malls in every city—the same chains, the same products. This goes even deeper than the trouble with import-replacing, because it means that new things are not being produced locally—things that can be improvements or different in any way. There is a sameness—this is one of the things that is boring people, this sameness. This sameness has economic implications: you don't get new products and services out of sameness. This means that somehow there isn't opportunity for these thousands flowers to bloom anymore.

KUNSTLER: The million flowers are now blooming in China. I don't know about you—every product I pick up is made in China. I'm not against the Chinese. But it makes you wonder how long we go on having an advanced civilization without making anything anymore. Can we?

JACOBS: I don't think so.

KUNSTLER: It seems to me that what we are doing is we are buying a lot of stuff from other people by basically running up tremendous, unprecedented amounts of debt. That can only go on so long.

JACOBS: But you know, we aren't complete dolts in all of this. For example, we don't manufacture our own computers. They are made mostly in Taiwan, but they aren't designed in Taiwan.

KUNSTLER: We hand them a set of blueprints, and they make the stuff for us.

JACOBS: There are still an awful lot of intelligent, clever, constructive Americans, and they are still doing clever, constructive things. Is it more necessary to be able to design computers, or is it more necessary to be able to manufacture computers? I think that it is necessary to do both. I think it is fatal to specialize. And all kinds of things show us that, and that the more diverse we are in what we can do, the better. But I don't think that you can dispose of the constructive and inventive things that America is doing and say "oh, we aren't doing anything anymore, and we are living off of what the poor Chinese do." It is more complicated than that. There is the example of Detroit, which you noticed yourself was once a very prosperous and diverse city. And look what happened when it just specialized in automobiles. Look at Manchester, when it specialized in those dark satanic mills, in textiles. It was supposed to be the city of the future.

KUNSTLER: We have an awful lot of places in America that don't specialize in anything anymore and don't produce anything in particular anymore.

JACOBS: Well, that's better than specializing.

KUNSTLER: I am thinking about the region where I live, which is a kind of a mini rust-belt of upstate New York—one town after another where the economy has completely vanished. There is no more Utica, New York, really. There is no more Amsterdam, New York, or Glens Falls, or Hudson Falls. They are gone. And I am wondering: is the rest of America going to be like that.

JACOBS: Never underestimate the power of a city to regenerate.

KUNSTLER: Well, that's fair enough.

JACOBS: And things everywhere are not as bad as you are picturing.

KUNSTLER: Oh, I am Mr. Gloom and Doom.

JACOBS: For instance, Portland. Lots of constructive things are happening in Portland.

KUNSTLER: I'd say Portland is in pretty good shape compared to lots of other American cities—but it ain't France.

JACOBS: No, it ain't. But there are lots of things about America that are better in their own way than France.

KUNSTLER: I am depressing myself. Are there other parts of the world, in Europe or elsewhere, that you particularly love or admire?

JACOBS: I am very fond of the Netherlands. My husband and I spent four weeks just traveling around there because I went to the Netherlands to make some talks and got paid. And we used the pay to travel.

KUNSTLER: So what rang your bell about it?

JACOBS: Actually, the immense variety of it on a very small compass. The human scale of the whole thing and the density is far above what we are used to in North America, or anywhere. The high density and human scale are not incompatible at all.

KUNSTLER: How do you feel about Paris?

JACOBS: I haven't been there long. I have only made short visits, but what I saw, of course, was enchanting. And I kept thinking that I had been there before. It was because I had seen it in paintings—all these triangular corners.

KUNSTLER: The urbanism is so rigorous. But as I have joked to lecture audiences before, nobody ever comes home from Paris and complains about the uniformity of the boulevards.

JACOBS: No, they are interesting, and they are beautiful.

KUNSTLER: What is your take on London?

JACOBS: I'm ambivalent about London because I'm so ambivalent about England in general.

KUNSTLER: Really? What's your beef with it?

JACOBS: I cannot stand that class system. I haven't been there in quite a few years, though I have been invited there often— I just don't want to go back. It's a kind of museum piece of feudalism as I can see, socially. The English rub me the wrong way—but I love Ireland.

KUNSTLER: I was there a few years ago. Ireland is sort of a strange case, because here you have this country that was miserably poor for hundreds and hundreds of years, and all of a sudden they have a middle class for the first time in their history. Well, one of the consequences, of course, is that there are unbelievable numbers of German tour buses clogging up their roads.

JACOBS: Yeah, no doubt. But it's a lovely place, and they are a lovely people. And maybe part of my animus against the English is the way they have always treated the Irish, and the way they still think about the Irish.

KUNSTLER: Have you been to South America or Mexico? I was in Mexico City a couple of years ago. Unbelievable.

JACOBS: What did you think of it?

KUNSTLER: The biggest ashtray in the world. And ecological horror—just on the ground. And I'll admit it was a social horror as well. I went out to visit the slums of Chalco, where more than a million people live in packing crates with mud floors. And it happens to be a part of the valley of Mexico that has very poor hydrology, and all the sewage from Mexico City proper percolates up in that part of the slum, and the people walk around in it in the rainy season in the mud, and then it dries out and turns into airborne disease. It's a pretty horrifying place. Any other places that you favor in the world?

JACOBS: I liked what I saw of Italy, which wasn't very much.

Of course, I was enchanted with Venice. I like Denmark. I shouldn't say Denmark, because the only part I have been in is Copenhagen.

KUNSTLER: The Europeans seem to have a higher regard for city life then we do, and to do better with it. How do you account for that?

JACOBS: Well, you have to go back to something I don't understand and can't explain, which are these hysterias that went over America. I guess different kinds of hysterias swept over Europe, but not that kind.

KUNSTLER: They get Adolf Hitler, and we get Ed Logue.

JACOBS: So we are lucky.

KUNSTLER: But you go to an Italian city and whenever I think about Italian cities, I think of being in a place that is almost completely made of masonry, and here and there, just a little spot of color—a geranium or a petunia or a flower, and they do that so beautifully.

JACOBS: It counts for a lot—those little spots of greenery and color.

KUNSTLER: Yeah, they don't have to put in a $30,000 berm full of landscaping and juniper shrubs and palm trees.

JACOBS: There is Lisbon—and it's a very poor city in many ways, or it was when I was there. I guess it still is. So many charming things, so many interesting things.

KUNSTLER: Have you been to Las Vegas?

JACOBS: No, I haven't. My husband went there to a convention. He gave me quite a report.

KUNSTLER: Yeah, I wanted to cut my throat after being there for about five days. In fact, I paid extra to change my airplane ticket and leave a day early. It's pretty frightful.

JACOBS: I like Japan.

KUNSTLER: Tell me about Japan.

JACOBS: I was there in '72, so what I will tell you is very outdated. But what you were just saying about that one flower, that one tree—well the Japanese are virtuosos. They make just the little accent that makes all the difference. So much there is so beautiful—just a shop window display is a work of art. Just the way they make all kinds of things out of bamboo is so ingenious. Just the way this little bamboo drain or latch is so beautiful. The masonry around the streams that holds up the bank is beautiful—and not all one kind, and not just cement.

KUNSTLER: That's something that amazes me with the United States versus Europe. When we are faced with the task of fixing up a river bank—and many American cities are on rivers—we have to put a theme park there. We have to put up ball parks, aquariums, all this stuff. In Europe, they make granite embankments with a ramp or stairs down to the water, and it's beautiful.

• • •

KUNSTLER: When did your husband pass away?

JACOBS: In '96—four years ago.

KUNSTLER: How has it been for you?

JACOBS: Well, of course I miss him. I'm glad I'm a working person. I mean, I'm still interested in my work—I didn't lose interest in life or anything. Also, my children and other members of the family I'm very close to.

KUNSTLER: Your son lives up the block?

JACOBS: Down the block. It has to be down toward the lake. Everything goes down toward the lake.

KUNSTLER: You have pretty clearly left urbanism somewhat behind and moved onto economics in the last fifteen or twenty years. What are you working on now?

JACOBS: I am not working on a book right now. Because I postpone—I get absolutely ruthless in my own way about not doing anything else when I am trying to concentrate on writing a book. I have to stick to it and concentrate. So all kinds of things that I should have been doing have been postponed. And I have been trying to catch up on them. I try to keep active as a citizen here, and do what I can.

KUNSTLER: Is there a particular idea that you're interested or turning over in your head, the way you were elaborating import-replacing twenty years ago, or the way you developed *Systems of Survival*? Is there a particular idea that you find you are galvanized by these days?

JACOBS: I am interested in the subject, for instance, of why time is such an enemy in American neighborhoods—what specific things at present does time threaten—and how can it be made an ally.

KUNSTLER: Are you suggesting that American neighborhoods by and large don't regenerate themselves?

JACOBS: I think that they have a very poor track record with regard to time.

KUNSTLER: How has Greenwich Village fared over the fifty, sixty years that you have known it?

JACOBS: Oh, it has done very well. If other city neighborhoods had done as well there would be no trouble in cities. There are too few neighborhoods right now, so the supply doesn't nearly meet the demand. So they are just gentrifying in the most ridiculous way. They are crowding out everybody except people with exorbitant amounts of money. Which is a symptom that demand for such a neighborhood has far out-stripped the supply.

KUNSTLER: I have always been puzzled why Harlem was not redeveloped. I went to high school in Harlem on 135th Street.

JACOBS: It is starting to. What I read is and hear is that it is starting to gentrify, but I am glad to see that it is black professionals and black families and artists that are leading in the gentrification. It would be too bad for the neighborhood to be taken away from them.

KUNSTLER: When I was a kid, Brooklyn was like another planet. It was like Czechoslovakia—it was so far away, and so alien. And now Brooklyn is the place where my whole generation has moved to in New York City.

JACOBS: Well, parts of Brooklyn now are, you might say, the outliers of Greenwich Village.

KUNSTLER: Was Greenwich Village ever a bad neighborhood, going back before your lifetime?

JACOBS: You know, it's not small. Greenwich Village is a pretty big district. And yes, there were parts of it. There was the south village, which was heavily Italian, and before that, I guess, mainly Irish. Carmine Street and so on. That was considered bad. Sullivan Street, which is considered very chic now—I remember it when it was just teeming with poor children and tenements, so I suppose it was considered bad. And of course, the West Village was considered bad. We didn't know it when we moved there, fortunately, but it was designated a slum to be cleared away in the 1930s, and Rexford Tugwell—who was one of Roosevelt's "brain trusters"—I think he was chairman of the planning commission at the time that was declared.

JACOBS: [*leafing through scrapbook, points at photograph*] Oh, here is Lewis Mumford! [*There are several letters accompanying it.*]

JACOBS: I am going to read this, so that we could get this on tape:

3 May 1958, Amenia, New York

Dear Jacobs,

Your talk at the New School gave me the deepest satisfaction perhaps because you stated with such refreshing clarity a point of view that only a few people in city planning circles like Ed Bacon even dimly understand. Your analysis of the functions of the city is sociologically of the first order. And none of the millions being squandered by the Ford Foundation or "urban research" will produce anything that has a minute fraction of your insight and common sense. Your analysis of the vast bungle called Lincoln Center is devastatingly just. I myself had held off attacking it in the New Yorker *because I mistakenly felt that even in an age as irrational as ours a plan as massively inept as that one would never get beyond the stage of advanced publicity. But I did not reckon with our present American capacity for organizing and capitalizing emptiness. You ought to reach a wider audience for your ideas. Have you thought of the* Saturday Evening Post? *They seem in the mood for serious contributions these days. At all events keep hammering. Your worst opponents are the old fogies who imagine that Le Corbusier is the last work in urbanism.*

    With all good wishes faithfully,
    Lewis Mumford

P.S. You are Miss, aren't you? I am nervous ever since I addressed a Japanese teacher of home economics as Miss and found out that she was a Mr.

                 18 June 1958, Amenia, New York
Dear Jacobs,

Always do what you would really like to do. There are a half a dozen publishers who would snap up a manuscript of yours on the city. And though I can't guess how the public would take to it, you have a duty to produce the book. There is no one else who had so many fresh and sensible things to say about the city and it is high time these things were said and discussed. So get to work. But have a contract sewed up after you have done a chapter or two. I am now finishing the first draft of volume one of my new book on cities, the historic part—I shan't finish the second volume on what to do about it until your work is done.

    Faithfully,
    Lewis Mumford

22 July 1958, Amenia, New York

These are the days dear Jane Jacobs when we have reason to fear the worst—both from city hall and from the White House. People suspect me of exaggeration I suppose when I suggest that if anything survives this age it will be known retrospectively as the age of wreckers and exterminators. Perhaps the greatest merit of the book I am now doing will be to show how we got this way. That may give us a clue to constructive counteractivism. But it is a long way from being finished, for the trail is both devious and dim. Meanwhile it is good news to learn of your own prospects. This own master builders unlike Ibsen's likes to hear the younger generation knocking at the door.

Faithfully Lewis Mumford

KUNSTLER: Where does he start knocking you?

JACOBS: This is the last one, and it's not to me.

KUNSTLER: This is to Mr. Wensburg of Columbia University:

Dear Mr. Wensburg,

I appreciate your courtesy in sending me Jacobs article which in fact I had happened to had already read. But in asking for comment you were in effect suggesting that an old surgeon give public judgement on the work of a confident but sloppy novice operating to remove an imaginary tumor to which the youngster has erroneously attributed the patient's affliction, whilst overlooking major

*impairments in the actual organs. Surgery has no useful contri-
bution to make in such a situation, except to sew up the patient
and dismiss the bungler.*

*Cordially yours,
[signed] Lewis Mumford*

THE LAST INTERVIEW

INTERVIEW BY ROBIN PHILPOT
FROM *THE QUESTION OF SEPARATISM*
(BARAKA BOOKS, 2011)
MAY 2, 2005

Twenty-five years after *The Question of Separatism* appeared and ten years after Quebec's second referendum on sovereignty in 1995, Jane Jacobs graciously agreed to an interview about Quebec and her book. The interview was conducted in her home on Albany Street, in Toronto's Annex district. Jane Jacobs talked freely for more than two hours with a forty-five minute break while she underwent physiotherapy for a hip ailment.

• • •

PHILPOT: How did people react to your 1979 Massey lectures and to the book, which came out in favour of sovereignty-association? Did the book get the coverage it deserved at the time?

JACOBS: Reactions were from Anglophones. I'm one. But I'm terrible at French. In fact, there was practically no reaction. My husband was a hospital architect and he was working on some hospitals in Alberta, and I told him to try to find out what they thought about separatism. He would come back on weekends. He said "well, I think I found out how they feel about separatism. I brought it up at lunch in the cafeteria, and everybody at the table was silent and then somebody said, 'Let's change the subject.'" The best thing is not to think about it. They don't even want to engage in talking pros and cons and why people feel this way.

PHILPOT: Does that explain the lack of reaction to your Massey Lectures and your book?

JACOBS: It's the same attitude. Don't want to think about it. It's an unwelcome subject.

PHILPOT: What do you attribute that attitude to?

JACOBS: It's fear. And this I don't have to guess at. Because there were lots of programs over the course of the two referendums and the general tenor of them was that if Quebec were to separate, then Canada would disintegrate. So that was the fear that there would be no identity anymore, for Canada. It was foolish, because there are so many examples of separatism, and nothing has disintegrated, unless they went to war.

PHILPOT: Do you mean that disintegration occurs when people go to war to oppose it?

JACOBS: There are a great many cases, I was counting them up to myself the other day, and couldn't even count the ones in central Asia, so many, and they end in *stan*. But even discounting those, there were over thirty of these cases in very recent times since Quebec, since the issue of Quebec was raised 1980.

So we have to ask: what's going on here? Why? I don't think this is pure coincidence. It's a phenomenon and it's widespread and it's so deeply felt. And there are so many different reasons the people feel to explain why they want to separate. But what do they have in common? And what is it all about? The world is usually not like this.

So trying to put together what they do have in common and what they don't have in common, here's what I come to. It's feedback from the world of some kind. What they have in common is that larger units are not satisfying people, they feel that these are out of control and what they seem to want in common and what they're happy about when they get it, and they calm down, which they do if they're not taken to war, is the satisfaction at last at having their own sovereignty.

You have to take examples. All except the would-be controlling states are very happy about this outcome. In the Balkans for instance, take the whole break-up of Serbia. The only people who are unhappy about it are the Serbs and they're unhappy because they're not in control of all these others any more.

But the Slovenes, the Croatians, the rest of them are very glad to be independent.

PHILPOT: So the danger is the will to control of would-be controlling states?

JACOBS: Yes and they're the ones that make war.

PHILPOT: Do you see Canada as a state that tends to control on this question?

JACOBS: Sure. English Canada has always wanted to control French Canada. English Canada conquered French Canada. So let's face the fact that this is a conquered country, and conquered countries often never forget what happened to them. Neither the conquered nor the conqueror ever really forget.

Now, I wrote about Norway. Norway was the very early example. And Norway and Sweden behaved in a wonderfully civilized manner. They could easily have gone to war. Tensions were very stressful prior to 1905. The other example of a very early case was in the United States, which was its own secession movement. And that did lead to war, the most humanly destructive war that the United States has ever had. The highest death rate. That has never been forgotten. There it was in the last election. The most recent election. [2004] There's still the confederacy and the union. Wars don't settle these things.

PHILPOT: Violent or autocratic ways of opposing do not settle these things?

JACOBS: No. And the victor in these things always thinks they will but they never do.

PHILPOT: Is the Irish question similar where the British thought they would solve the problem by partitioning Ireland?

JACOBS: Yes, and they didn't solve it.

•   •   •

PHILPOT: You make a convincing case about the similarities between Sweden/Norway and Canada/Quebec. You write: "To its great credit Sweden neither then nor afterward banned the Storting or tried to suppress its elections, never attempted to censor its debates or interfere in its communications with the Norwegian people, and did not poison Norwegian political life with spies and secret police or corrupt it with bribes and informers." Can we say the same thing about Canada?

JACOBS: No!

PHILPOT: Please expand.

JACOBS: Well, let's see: in those indictments you can't level at Sweden, they never tried to ban the constitution or undermine the settlement that they wanted. Well you can't say that of Canada. Any indication of revolt on the part of Quebec was either bought off, with a good deal of corruption—this is not a new thing [*reference to the sponsorship scandal*]*—or suppressed in some other way. And very often by trying to, and succeeding in, undermining the self-confidence of Quebecers. That's exactly what [Pierre] Trudeau did. That was his whole method. And unfortunately [René] Lévesque had so little self-confidence in Quebec and in the people themselves, that he fell for that and, yes, he'd say, you know, it might be ruinous for us economically.

* The interview was conducted shortly after public hearings held by the Commission of Inquiry into the Sponsorship Program and Advertising Activities, known as the Gomery Commission. The "sponsorship scandal," which rocked the Government of Canada led by Jean Chrétien, revealed that millions of dollars were funneled into Quebec to promote "Canadian identity" over Quebec identity. Leaders of Canada's Liberal Party and PR firms linked to it had also set up a kickback scheme to help fund election campaigns.

PHILPOT: So he fell for that because he lacked confidence in the Quebec people?

JACOBS: Yes, and also because he didn't understand why things do collapse. It's usually a very banal reason why things do collapse. It's not a grand reason why they collapse economically, at least in the West. The reason is usually that the entrepreneurial investors of the time just want to repeat themselves indefinitely and don't know when to stop. You can't do that. And so finally the housing boom, or the auto boom, or whatever it is that's been carrying things along, runs out of customers.

PHILPOT: And they haven't planned renewal or replacement?

JACOBS: Actually, replacement is not planned, it just happens. But they haven't found ways to encourage it. In fact they find ways to suppress the possibility of replacement. Just like the oil companies now going in for the oil sands and at the cost of God knows how much money. Think what that same amount of money and encouragement would do with non-fossil fuels. But no, no!

I was at a party sitting beside a guy involved in tar sands. A man from Edmonton. I asked him why he was so confident. He said it was because of the price of oil. Then I asked if he would advise a young person to get involved in it for the rest of his life. Why was he confident? Well, he said, because China was interested. I replied: you know China has gotten into a lot of things that were wrong in the past century. Why are you so confident? Well he just is. He has an exploitative attitude towards China. Maybe they are suckers, but we've got a good thing going for a while. He didn't say so in so many words.

PHILPOT: You don't think he should be so confident?

JACOBS: No. I think the fundamentals are against the success. The very fact that it costs so much to develop. That's not an argument in favour of it. That's against the law of diminishing returns. You can't bank on diminishing returns.

PHILPOT: Are you an economist by training? What is your formal training?

JACOBS: Very little. After I graduated from High School in Scranton, Pennsylvania, I didn't want to go to school any more. I was tired of school. I was getting very rebellious about it. My parents said I didn't have to go to college. They said they had saved money if I wanted to, but that I didn't have to want to I think that was very good. And after a few years of working, five years of work—I was a young worker—but I could work as a secretary because I had learned touch typing. I had also gotten out of school in February, and so I had half a year for business school and so I learned a little more, and I was equipped to get a job as a secretary. So I went to New York. Also because Scranton was a coal town—anthracite coal, superior coal. There were laws in New York that it was the only kind of coal that could be sold. During the First World War, all those regulations had been broken. So Scranton was in a depression on that account, soon after the First World War and well before the great depression set in.

PHILPOT: So you're self educated? All your theories and books, you've worked on that alone?

JACOBS: And with help from other people.

PHILPOT: In your recent book *Dark Age Ahead*, you have a chapter entitled "Credentialing Versus Education." You feel that "credentialism" has been bad for education and prevents people from having the curiosity and the intellectual probity that allow them to develop new ideas.

JACOBS: I've gotten more and more radical on this myself. I have an entirely new hypothesis on how economies, macro-economies, form themselves and organize themselves, and where this kind of life comes from. But it's so different from the standard idea of economic life. But some people believe it because, for one thing, I haven't made up my new hypothesis, which I call "uncovering the economy." Everything in the hypothesis is out there, happening, and it accounts for so many things that are just slid over and ignored in regular economics. But I don't know, yes I do know why I do it. It's interesting in the first place; I think truth is more interesting than baloney.

PHILPOT: The original Massey lectures were entitled "Canadian Cities and Sovereignty Association." In those lectures and in the book you come to support sovereignty because of your idea of how cities work. Do you think that what you wrote in 1980 about Montreal and Toronto has proven to be true? You posit that Quebec's need for Montreal to be a metropolis independent of Toronto requires that Quebec be able to operate independently. Do you think that still applies today?

JACOBS: Yes. And I think it is partly because of currencies, national currencies. And Toronto does swing the Canadian national currency, and that's often to the detriment, nobody's intention, just the automatic detriment to the cities it trades with.

PHILPOT: Because the value of the currency is established by what goes on in Toronto? So you favour a Quebec currency, though the way things are going with the Euro, would you still favour a Quebec currency?

JACOBS: Yes. And I think it's a mistake for the Europeans, the Western European countries, to blot out so many currencies in favour of who knows which one is going to win out. Maybe Frankfurt. It will not favour all the other countries. Europe had something really wonderful going for it with the different currencies. Look at all the development in Europe over so many centuries, and yes they got into these wars and that pretty well ruined it. They also had an awful lot of relationships which didn't involve fighting each other, but involved learning from each other, and building on each other's successes.

PHILPOT: If you were in France now would you vote in favour of the European Constitution or against it?*

* A referendum was held in France on May 29, 2005, three weeks after the interview. 56.8 percent of French voters voted No in opposition to the European Constitution.

JACOBS: I would be against it. But I don't see much use in being against it unless there's a great deal of talk and debate about it so that people are educated as to why, otherwise into the vacuum will come really nasty reasons of hatred and bigotry, etc.

PHILPOT: You get interviewed frequently by the media. Do they ask you about Quebec?

JACOBS: No. Practically never. You're the first one!

PHILPOT: Yet there are very few books in English that broach the subject as you do?

JACOBS: In my research, I couldn't find any in English that went into it.

PHILPOT: So people are not interested in knowing why you reached this conclusion. Do you know Montreal very well?

JACOBS: Not well. I've been there a few times. I think in Quebec journalists were a bit interested. Elsewhere no.

PHILPOT: Do you think that with the new buzzword of "Globalization" the situation has changed since the 1980s?

JACOBS: No. You know people ignore the common threads that run through economic life and we're still in the primitive early stages of these things. Globalization is one of the first things that ever showed up. Way back when trade began to revive after the Dark Ages, it was very international. Sardinia sold cheese to every European city and every available market, and nothing but cheese. I call places like that "supply regions." And I give an example of how powerful the force is when a lot of cities act as one, which they do, in getting what they want rom a supply region.

PHILPOT: So this idea of globalization where the markets become international, it's basically the continuation of what's gone on?

JACOBS: Yes, globalization has gone on since around 1200 or so. It went on in classical times, before the Dark Age.

• • •

PHILPOT: You are originally from the United States. How would you say the United States will react to a sovereign Quebec?

JACOBS: I think that people in Canada who are frightened may be right to the extent that the United States will try to take advantage of this and aggrandize and maybe scare Canadians into falling in with their plans. After all the United States is irked with Canada these days because it hasn't fallen in with its war in Iraq.

PHILPOT: So the United States could try to take advantage of a weakened Canada?

JACOBS: They could try.

PHILPOT: You don't see that as inevitable?

JACOBS: No. And if it does do that, if they succeed in it, it will be only if Canada is so scared and docile that it allows it to happen.

PHILPOT: I've interviewed people with political power in English Canada for a book and they've said that Quebec cannot separate from Canada, because Canada would disappear. You don't give any credence to that unless Canada decides to give up?

JACOBS: Yes. Exactly. But of course, countries do that sometimes; they decide to give up. I feel some urgency in my new hypothesis, yet I'm so dubious it will be accepted. If it is, the wrong kinds of reasons will explain why it is accepted. So why bother, why interfere?

Well, I've had to ask myself that. Ordinary people are capable of wonderful economic things without even knowing they're doing wonderful things. You know, the next thing is not planned. It just seems to happen. It is very seldom planned.

I would like it to be understood, and increasingly understood as time passes, that all our human economic achievements have been done by ordinary people, not by exceptionally educated people, or by elites, or by supernatural forces, for heaven's sake. Yet without understanding this, people are all too willing to fall for the idea that they can't do this, they themselves, or anybody they know, because they're too ordinary.

PHILPOT: Their own self-image stops them from seeing that they can do something?

JACOBS: Yes.

PHILPOT: Do you think that is what happened to René Lévesque? That it was a lack of confidence in what he could have accomplished with the Quebec people?

JACOBS: Yes.

PHILPOT: In your book *Dark Age Ahead*, you also talk of subsidiarity and fiscal accountability. Very interesting points! They too would argue once again in favour of Quebec sovereignty.

JACOBS: Absolutely. Look how the inability to face [the Gomery Commission and the sponsorship scandal] and solve this in a civilized way is corrupting the whole country.

PHILPOT: Please expand.

JACOBS: Well, one way that English Canada, or English authorities, or frightened authorities operating in Quebec, have tried to put this whole thing to rest, and say it's all settled, which it obviously is not, is to try to buy off Quebec. That seems the most promising way, more than the use of force. Trudeau, as I mentioned, managed this quite well. And it's the way of selling Quebec. Forget about sovereignty. Show them that their interest is somewhere else, their economic interest.

It's largely a matter of buying Quebec. Well when you buy people, and particularly try to change their deep principles by buying them, it becomes very corrupt, automatically, by the nature of the transaction. They have to be kidded about what's happening to them.

Now a friend of mine who's been making some business trips to Montreal and has visited some of the sessions [of the Gomery Commission], says that it's very instructive to watch the Quebecers, and see how furious they are. Their faces are so set, they're not enjoying this, they're so angry. So I say, what are they angry at? In fact, they realize they've been had. They realize for the first time, they've been had over and over again in the past.

PHILPOT: Would you agree that what the Liberal Party has been doing with the sponsorships is by no means a trivial matter?

JACOBS: Yes. It's been their policy. It continues to be their policy. They'll continue to do it. It's all they know how to do. And I even see what will be the way.

PHILPOT: What will it be?

JACOBS: You'll think I'm crazy. I think that the federal government, which needs an awful lot of largesse for this kind of thing—and can't depend so much on getting unlimited amounts for it out of Toronto—has got a new idea. And I'll tell you in a bare-faced manner what I think the idea is, and then I'll tell you what I think the evidence shows.

I think that it's going in for a national plan of gambling finance. And the evidence for this: well, first it's all rumours and whispers. We had a big fight here that resulted in a change of mayor: whether Toronto Island should be developed, with a bridge. It made no economic nor transportation sense, but it could be done by the federal government, because it has a port authority and it's an absurd port authority.

There would be economic things it could do that would be useful—i.e., a landing place for a ferry from Rochester. This was treated as something that should be brushed off. No convenience, amenities, or respect. That's rather odd. Why would they behave like that, and then want to pour money into the island and the bridge? The whisper is that it never could pay off as a sensible plan of transportation, but the idea is that it would be a fine place to develop casinos. And the airport would be part of it. The junketeers—gambling junketeers—could come directly, and it would be a gold mine. It would be run by the federal government, in international waters: a port authority has all the legal hold on it that it needs.

It could raise money to buy Quebec, and for other purposes. Whatever the federal government needs money for, lots of money. At the same time there's a transportation plan in British Columbia, which is silly and goes absolutely against what the present premier has said in the past about a highway and highways in Vancouver. So a lot of pressure has been going on.

•   •   •

PHILPOT: What are you working on now?

JACOBS: The name of my upcoming book will be *Uncovering the Economy* in 2006. And the next book ought to be a really fun one to write. It will be, *A Sad But Short Biography of the Human Race*. So far short. It's not my anticipation that we're into evolution for a short run, it will be long, but it's been short up till now. And we're much closer to our beginnings than we realize. We think we're so advanced.

I think that I was saying our economies haven't changed since the beginning and certainly globalization is not a new thing.

PHILPOT: Why do you think that economists, politicians and public people bandy the word globalization about so much? This is a major change in discourse.

JACOBS: They love to think that things have changed so that they can forget all their mistakes and not have to explain them any more: oh well because of globalization, the web, etc.

PHILPOT: Do you think the web has the effect of bringing people together or keeping people apart?

JACOBS: It brings some people together but it keeps others apart, just like language, just like other types of communication. And it's not nearly as revolutionary as language itself.

PHILPOT: Comparable to the printing press?

JACOBS: I don't think it's as important as that. Because with the printing press, just think what that meant to communications, and how fast it happened. There were sixty new publishers in Vienna, I think, in no time. And this had not been planned by anybody. One of these enormous changes that just seemed to occur when their time has come. When ordinary people start doing something, they don't really know that it's happening.

PHILPOT: When you say "anecdotal evidence is the only real evidence," what do you mean?

JACOBS: What other kind of evidence is there? There is statistical evidence in economics. But when do people get interested enough to do statistics? If you don't count things, you never have them. That's the problem. There hasn't been enough interest to count what should be counted.

PHILPOT: People don't count the things that need to be counted?

JACOBS: Right, because they're not interested. They only get interested based on anecdotal evidence. That's the only evidence there is until people begin to get interested.

PHILPOT: And even statistical evidence is based on anecdotes, because statistical evidence is based on the story of somebody doing something . . .

JACOBS: And whatever it may be, it may be very tenuous, something that economists already do, like counting the amount of money in circulation. But why do they care? Some anecdote has piqued their curiosity.

PHILPOT: In political economy and political science, everything appears based on polls these days. Don't you find that that flies in the face of what you say about the importance of anecdotal evidence? People bring out the latest poll to prove something.

JACOBS: And polls can be rigged according to the kind of question is asked. But some sort of anecdotal evidence has piqued the curiosity to ask the question. 61 percent of Canadians believe bla-bla. Where did the idea of bla-bla come from? The all-powerful creator? It comes form stories that people tell.

PHILPOT: You make that point strongly in *Dark Age Ahead* in the wake of the heat wave in Chicago?*

JACOBS: That man who did that study, did it all based on anecdotal evidence. The statistical evidence that existed was the wrong statistical evidence when they began to compile it. It was just noise.

PHILPOT: They didn't ask the right questions, and they tried to prove something so they could blame the victim?

---

* In *Dark Age Ahead*, Jane Jacobs contrasts an official study whose "findings are worse than useless" on the high number of deaths among the elderly poor in Chicago during a heat wave with that of a young sociology graduate who then published a book titled *Heat Wave, A Social Autopsy of a Disaster in Chicago*, University of Chicago Press (2003). The young sociology graduate "spoke with fresh truths drawn from the real world," according to Jacobs.

JACOBS: And I've never gotten any feedback from that. And I think that it's quite revealing, that Chicago thing. The problem in Chicago was due to "credentialism." It was prescribed and the wrong prescription. But all those who did the study had their credentials.

PHILPOT: The Yes side campaigned in the 1995 Quebec referendum on the slogan "Oui et ça devient possible," "Vote yes and it will be possible." Symbols or images of peace, work, flowers or a map of the world represented what would be possible. In your opinion, what would become possible if Quebec were sovereign?

JACOBS: Well. Lots of things are not possible for municipalities, suburbs, or collections of them now. They are not possible and they would become possible, because they would have more authority. They would have the same authority as a province now.

PHILPOT: If Quebec became sovereign, Montreal and Quebec City would be granted greater powers?

JACOBS: Yes well, there would be one level of government that would be missing, one less level of government. The municipality would become the second level.

One of our troubles now is that we try to make municipalities that are totally different from each other all act as if they were the same kind of creature, with the same kinds of possibilities. Not so. Some of the large ones in Quebec can contain within them most of the answers to their own practical problems. And so lots of different possibilities for doing things in a practical and different way become available.

It's not true of very small places. They just don't have the skills, the connections, the diversity.

PHILPOT: You refer to Montreal's becoming a regional city with regard to Toronto. If Quebec were sovereign, would Montreal take on a different role within Quebec?

JACOBS: Just the way in Europe, Paris, Copenhagen, and Stockholm, and Frankfurt, possibly, and Berlin, certainly, all had important roles, because of independence. Because they were depending on themselves.

PHILPOT: Not feeders for another metropolis?

JACOBS: You see, cities never flourish alone. They have to be trading with other cities. My new hypothesis shows why. But also in trading with each other they can't be in too different stages of development, and they can't copy one another. Backward cities, or younger cities, or newly forming cities in supply regions, have to develop to a great extent on one another's shoulders. This is one of the terrible things about empires. Empires want them only to trade with the empire, which doesn't help them at all. It's just a way of exploiting them.

PHILPOT: Would you describe the logic of the relationship between Toronto and Montreal, the Golden Horseshoe and Quebec, as one that resembles that of an empire?

JACOBS: Yes!

PHILPOT: The way to break that logic is for Quebec to become independent and be able to trade equally with Toronto? You also say we have to stop fantasizing that English Canada could shut out Quebec as the United States did to Cuba because it would be harmful for everybody?

JACOBS: Sure it would be harmful. A good trading situation can't be done without a certain amount of independence. It can't be done constructively. Instead of being a win-win situation, which a good trading situation is, it becomes too competitive, it becomes a lose-win situation, maybe even a lose-lose situation.

PHILPOT: You mean if there's not a cooperative situation established?

JACOBS: In its very essence, healthy trade is a win-win situation. When people who get their jollies and interest out of life by fighting only with other people, they're very poor traders. They only want to dominate, instead of finding a way that everybody benefits. So in that sense, globalization is not the same as it was in some innocence past.

PHILPOT: Because globalization has come to involve domination?

JACOBS: It's come more and more to involve domination. And that doesn't work and so the imperial power, which is now the U.S., collapses.

PHILPOT: Do you foresee that?

JACOBS: Yes.

PHILPOT: What kind of horizon?

JACOBS: The collapse will start out as a banal thing . . . These investing entrepreneurs want to keep doing the same thing they've always been doing. There aren't enough customers for condominiums at one point. So it gets to be a business cycle. An interesting thing thing about business cycles is that they don't exist in small or backward economies. They only exist in city economies, in advanced economies, and that's an interesting thing. Why is it? Another thing to *Uncover the Economy* to find out. It's the same in that respect as the explosive growth in cities. Things have reasons for being.

Economics, orthodox economics, is a travesty, a joke. Nothing to do with reality, it has to do with wishes. What we wish the economy to be. It's not related to what we see in real life, or explaining any of these mysteries.

PHILPOT: You wrote *The Question of Separatism, Quebec and the Struggle over Sovereignty* in 1979 and 1980. If you were to write it again today, would you come to the same conclusions?

JACOBS: Yes, not because it's in my head, but because that's the way it is in the world, and it still holds.

JANE JACOBS (1916–2006) was born in Scranton, Pennsylvania, in 1916, the daughter of a doctor and a nurse. After graduating from high school, she briefly worked as an unpaid assistant at *The Scranton Tribune*, before moving to New York City in 1934, where she worked as a secretary and freelance writer, and took classes at Columbia University's School of General Studies. In 1952, she became a staff writer at *Architectural Forum*, and in 1961, she published *The Death and Life of Great American Cities*, a stinging but prescriptive critique of midcentury architectural norms that would become one of the twentieth century's most influential books of urban planning. The impact of *Death and Life* on the fields of planning, architecture, and urban sociology has been massive, and the book later became an inspiration for the field of New Urbanism. Jacobs was also an urban activist: in the 1950s and '60s, she fought proposals that would have transformed her neighborhood of Greenwich Village, including the planned Lower Manhattan Expressway. In later years, Jacobs wrote about the fields of economics and social relations; her other books include *Cities and the Wealth of Nations*, *The Question of Separatism*, and *Dark Age Ahead*. Jacobs and her family moved to Toronto in 1968, where she would live until her death in 2006.

EVE AUCHINCLOSS, a writer and editor, worked for *Mademoiselle* and *Connoisseur*, among other publications, and contributed to *The New York Review of Books*.

NANCY LYNCH contributed to *Mademoiselle*.

ROBERTA BRANDES GRATZ is an award-winning journalist and critic, and the author of *The Living City: Thinking Small in a Big Way*, *Cities Back From the Edge: New Life for Downtown*, *The Battle For Gotham: New York in the Shadow of Robert Moses and Jane Jacobs*, and, most recently, *We're Still Here Ya Bastards: How the People of New Orleans Rebuilt Their City*, among other books. Gratz served on the New York City Landmarks Preservation Committee between 2003 and 2010, and she is a cofounder, in collaboration with Jane Jacobs, of The Center for the Living City.

JAMES HOWARD KUNSTLER is the author of thirteen novels, including *World Made by Hand*, *The Witch of Hebron*, *The Harrows of*

Spring, and five nonfiction books, including *The Long Emergency* and *The Geography of Nowhere*. He has participated in TED conferences and lectured at Harvard, Yale, Columbia, Cornell, MIT, and many other colleges. He lives in upstate New York.

ROBIN PHILPOT is a writer, translator, and publisher of Baraka Books. He is the author of six books in French on international politics and on Quebec and Canadian political issues. He is the author of *Rwanda and the New Scramble for Africa*, and the coauthor of *A People's History of Quebec*. He lives in Montreal.

THE LAST INTERVIEW SERIES

KURT VONNEGUT: THE LAST INTERVIEW

"I think it can be tremendously refreshing if a creator of literature has something on his mind other than the history of literature so far. Literature should not disappear up its own asshole, so to speak."

$15.95 / $17.95 CAN
978-1-61219-090-7
ebook: 978-1-61219-091-4

LEARNING TO LIVE FINALLY: THE LAST INTERVIEW
JACQUES DERRIDA

"I am at war with myself, it's true, you couldn't possibly know to what extent ... I say contradictory things that are, we might say, in real tension; they are what construct me, make me live, and will make me die."

translated by PASCAL-ANNE BRAULT and MICHAEL NAAS

$15.95 / $17.95 CAN
978-1-61219-094-5
ebook: 978-1-61219-032-7

ROBERTO BOLAÑO: THE LAST INTERVIEW

"Posthumous: It sounds like the name of a Roman gladiator, an unconquered gladiator. At least that's what poor Posthumous would like to believe. It gives him courage."

translated by SYBIL PEREZ and others

$15.95 / $17.95 CAN
978-1-61219-095-2
ebook: 978-1-61219-033-4

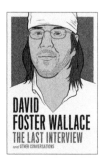

DAVID FOSTER WALLACE: THE LAST INTERVIEW

"I don't know what you're thinking or what it's like inside you and you don't know what it's like inside me. In fiction... we can leap over that wall itself in a certain way."

$15.95 / $15.95 CAN
978-1-61219-206-2
ebook: 978-1-61219-207-9

THE LAST INTERVIEW SERIES

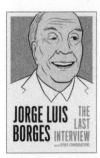

JORGE LUIS BORGES: THE LAST INTERVIEW

"Believe me: the benefits of blindness have been greatly exaggerated. If I could see, I would never leave the house, I'd stay indoors reading the many books that surround me."

translated by KIT MAUDE

$15.95 / $15.95 CAN
978-1-61219-204-8
ebook: 978-1-61219-205-5

HANNAH ARENDT: THE LAST INTERVIEW

"There are no dangerous thoughts for the simple reason that thinking itself is such a dangerous enterprise."

$15.95 / $15.95 CAN
978-1-61219-311-3
ebook: 978-1-61219-312-0

RAY BRADBURY: THE LAST INTERVIEW

"You don't have to destroy books to destroy a culture. Just get people to stop reading them."

$15.95 / $15.95 CAN
978-1-61219-421-9
ebook: 978-1-61219-422-6

JAMES BALDWIN: THE LAST INTERVIEW

"You don't realize that you're intelligent until it gets you into trouble."

$15.95 / $15.95 CAN
978-1-61219-400-4
ebook: 978-1-61219-401-1

THE LAST INTERVIEW SERIES

ERNEST HEMINGWAY: THE LAST INTERVIEW

"The most essential gift for a good writer is a built-in, shockproof, shit detector."

$15.95 / $20.95 CAN
978-1-61219-522-3
ebook: 978-1-61219-523-0

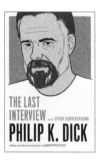

PHILIP K. DICK: THE LAST INTERVIEW

"The basic thing is, how frightened are you of chaos? And how happy are you with order?"

$15.95 / $20.95 CAN
978-1-61219-526-1
ebook: 978-1-61219-527-8

NORA EPHRON: THE LAST INTERVIEW

"You better *make* them care about what you think. It had better be quirky or perverse or thoughtful enough so that you hit some chord in them. Otherwise, it doesn't work."

$15.95 / $20.95 CAN
978-1-61219-524-7
ebook: 978-1-61219-525-4